From: **Badger Wildlife Management**
Bat Eviction Specialists!
Removal of Squirrels, Birds, Raccoons, etc.
320-250-5572   763-389-8887

THE DUCK COMMANDER Family

How Faith, Family, and Ducks Created a Dynasty

Willie and Korie Robertson

HOWARD BOOKS
A DIVISION OF SIMON & SCHUSTER, INC.
New York • Nashville • London • Toronto • Sydney • New Delhi

Howard Books
A Division of Simon & Schuster, Inc.
1230 Avenue of the Americas
New York, NY 10020

First Howard Books trade paperback edition August 2014

HOWARD and colophon are trademarks of Simon & Schuster, Inc.

For information about special discounts for bulk purchases,
please contact Simon & Schuster Special Sales at
1-866-506-1949 or business@simonandschuster.com.

The Simon & Schuster Speakers Bureau can bring authors to your live event.
For more information or to book an event, contact the Simon & Schuster Speakers
Bureau at 1-866-248-3049 or visit our website at www.simonspeakers.com.

Scripture quotations taken from THE HOLY BIBLE, NEW
INTERNATIONAL VERSION®, NIV® Copyright © 1973, 1978, 1984
by Biblica, Inc.™ Used by permission. All rights reserved worldwide.

Designed by Stephanie Walker

Manufactured in the United States of America

10 9 8 7 6 5 4 3 2 1

The Library of Congress has cataloged the hardcover edition as follows:
Robertson, Willie.
    The Duck Commander family : how faith, family, and ducks built a dynasty /
Willie and Korie Robertson.
        p. cm.
    1. Robertson, Willie, 1972–   2. Robertson, Willie, 1972—Family.   3. Television
personalities—United States—Biography.   4. Businessmen—United States—Biography.
5. Duck dynasty (Television program).   I. Robertson, Korie, 1973–   II. Title.
PN1992.4.R54A3 2012
791.4502'8092—dc23   2012030712
[B]

ISBN 978-1-4767-0354-1
ISBN 978-1-4767-0366-4 (pbk)
ISBN 978-1-4767-0362-6 (ebook)

For our parents,
Phil and Kay Robertson and John and Chrys Howard,
and
for our children,
John Luke, Sadie, Will, Bella, and Rebecca

Contents

Prologue: Born and "Corn" Bred 1

Chapter One: Rice 'n' Beans........................... 5

Chapter Two: Fried Bologna......................... 19

Chapter Three: Fried Catfish....................... 31

Chapter Four: Free Lunch 43

Chapter Five: Toast 'n' Pizza 55

Chapter Six: Roadkill................................ 73

Chapter Seven: Omelets.............................. 81

Chapter Eight: Chicken Strips 95

Chapter Nine: Duck Gumbo 107

Chapter Ten: Frog Legs.............................. 123

Chapter Eleven: Chicken Feet 143

Chapter Twelve: Fast Food 159

Chapter Thirteen: Fried Burgers 175

Chapter Fourteen: Dumplings, Hot Water,

    Cornbread, and Fried Squirrels.................... 193

Chapter Fifteen: Duck Wraps....................... 207

Chapter Sixteen: Back Straps 227

Chapter Seventeen: Duck and Dressing.............. 247

Acknowledgments 261

PROLOGUE

BORN AND "CORN" BRED

THESE COMMANDMENTS THAT I GIVE YOU TODAY ARE TO BE ON YOUR HEARTS. IMPRESS THEM ON YOUR CHILDREN. TALK ABOUT THEM WHEN YOU SIT AT HOME AND WHEN YOU WALK ALONG THE ROAD, WHEN YOU LIE DOWN AND WHEN YOU GET UP. TIE THEM AS SYMBOLS ON YOUR HANDS AND BIND THEM ON YOUR FOREHEADS. WRITE THEM ON THE DOORFRAMES OF YOUR HOUSES AND ON YOUR GATES.
—DEUTERONOMY 6:6–9

For as long as I can remember, my life has centered around three building blocks: faith, family, and food. The dinner table is where the Robertson family shares wisdom, confessions, laughter, faith, and dreams. This is family time, and I am thankful to have learned a good many important life lessons around that table.

Even before we started filming our family dinners for our TV show *Duck Dynasty,* I always thought of the Robertson dinner table as a stage in a Broadway play. Whoever was talking at the time had the spotlight and everyone else was the supporting cast. As kids, we learned about how to keep everyone's attention with a good story and about comedic timing.

1

This is also where we perfected the art of exaggeration. I think Kay's the best at it, or the worst, depending on which way you look at it. She can turn a simple story about her dog going missing for thirty minutes into a long gut-wrenching tale of love, loss, and everything in between. Along with the comedic moments, we've never lacked drama, either!

At the family table, I learned how to defend an argument and stand up for what I believe. The Robertson dinner table is like a weekly debate session. If you offer an opinion about something, you'd better be able to defend it. This is where we learned to argue passionately about our convictions, and the Robertson family, of course, has never been short on opinions. We have arguments about everything from crawfish pie to religion to shotguns. The debates can sometimes get loud, but they're never ugly or disrespectful. It's just that each of us feels very strongly about our beliefs, and we're not going to change our minds about something unless someone else offers a very good case to the contrary.

The dinner table is where I learned to follow my dreams. This is where Dad told us he was going to start Duck Commander, and where I told my family I was getting married and heading off to college. Our hopes and aspirations were never shot down, never debated, only encouraged. We might have been eating fried bologna at the time because that was all we could afford, but there was hope that one day we would be feasting on a big fat rib-eye steak. I remember one time around the dinner table Alan told my parents he wanted a Chevy Blazer. My dad said, "There will come a day where we'll all have Chevy Blazers!" He didn't actually tell Alan no; Phil was only telling all of us, "Have patience and believe." And we did, no matter how difficult things were.

At the dinner table we learned to respect our elders. In a lot of homes, the kids make their plates first, but it was never that way in the Robertson house. At our house, the kids always ate last. We would get what was left after the adults made their plates, which was usually a fried chicken neck and rarely a breast or thigh. But we learned to be thankful and content with what we had and that the world didn't revolve around us.

We learned to be hospitable. There were always extra faces around our family's table. No matter how little we had, we always had room to set out one more plate. If we had unexpected guests, Mom pulled out more meat from the freezer and added it to gumbo, or made another batch of her delicious biscuits. In the Robertson house, it's almost an unpardonable sin to not have enough food. Kay likes to say you never run out of three things: toilet paper, butter, or ketchup. But she stocks up on more than that. If the world is ever coming to an end, we're definitely going to Kay and Phil's house. That woman's got enough food in the freezer to live for months, and if we did run out, we could count on Phil to go catch something to fill our bellies.

We also learned that a good meal goes a long way. After Phil started Duck Commander, it didn't take him long to figure out food was a great way to get people to help. All of his workers loved to eat his ducks, crawfish dishes, fried fish, or whatever he or Kay was cooking that day. If a big order needed to be packed up to go out to a buyer, we'd have a fish fry and invite fifty people over. Mom and Dad would feed them and they'd be more than happy to pitch in. Phil and Kay never had to pay a dime; they just cooked for the crew, which always left our house full and happy, and left everyone hoping to be invited the next time we needed some extra help.

Back when Duck Commander was all being run out of Kay and Phil's house, my mom cooked lunch every day for our family and employees. Yes, times have changed. Now we couldn't even fit all of our employees in Mom and Dad's house! We've grown, but all of these lessons still remain. As Robertsons, we value the time around the table with our family; we are still trying to one-up each other with the best story, still defending the last stupid decision we made, and still laughing with one another and loving each other along the way.

1

RICE 'N' BEANS

CONSIDER IT PURE JOY, MY BROTHERS, WHENEVER YOU
FACE TRIALS OF MANY KINDS, BECAUSE YOU KNOW THAT THE
TESTING OF YOUR FAITH DEVELOPS PERSEVERANCE.
—JAMES 1:2–3

I know this might be hard to believe, but Phil was actually fishing when I was born. I was born on April 22, 1972, which was two days before Phil's birthday. I guess he was out celebrating a couple of days early because when I came into the world at Tri-Ward General Hospital in Bernice, Louisiana, Phil was sitting in a boat fishing for catfish at Bayou D'Arbonne Lake. I was the third of Phil and Kay's four sons, and Phil was only at the hospital to witness the birth of my youngest brother, Jeptha. Phil claims watching Jep's birth traumatized him so much that he wasn't sure he could ever have sex again. Of course, he says, it only took him about six weeks to get over it. I guess I'm just glad Phil was there nine months before I was born or I wouldn't be here today.

Phil likes to joke that he named me after one of his former students, who was a good football player but had failed the eighth grade three times. The truth is that I was named after Willie Ezell, my maternal grandfather, who passed away from a heart attack when Kay was only fourteen. I was born with very long, curly hair, and Kay joked that I looked a lot like the boxing promoter Don King. When Kay was getting ready to leave the hospital, they put me out in the hall with the other newborn babies. Sounds like a good chance for babies to get switched at birth to me, but apparently that's how they did it back then. Anyway, there was no chance of mistaking me for one of the other babies. People who walked by would stop, look at me, and then ask, "Who is that kid with all the hair?" They're still asking that same question about me today.

Phil was born and raised in Caddo Parish in Northwest Louisiana, near where the state converges with Arkansas and Texas. His father, James Robertson, was the son of Judge Euan Robertson, the longtime justice of the peace in Vivian, Louisiana. James Robertson married Merritt Hale; we always called them Pa and Granny.

Phil Alexander Robertson was born on the family's farm outside Vivian on April 24, 1946. Phil had four brothers and two sisters, and they spent much of their childhood living in an old log house located on land owned by Pa's aunt Myrtle Gauss. The cabin was pretty rustic and didn't even have indoor plumbing. But the log house came with more than four hundred acres, which is where Phil and his brothers learned to hunt and fish. The woods surrounding the farm were filled with squirrels, quail, and doves, and the Robertson boys could hunt for duck and fish for white perch and bream at nearby Black Bayou and Caddo Lake.

Pa started working in the oil industry when he was young, after black gold was discovered in East Texas and at the Caddo Pine Island Oil Field in Caddo Parish in the early twentieth century.

When Phil was in high school, his family was forced to move because Aunt Myrtle sold her farm. They relocated to Dixie, Louisiana, which is about fifteen miles north of Shreveport. Granny had suffered a nervous breakdown and was diagnosed with manic depression. Pa hoped the move would stabilize Granny's condition. She was twice confined to the Louisiana mental institute at Pineville, where she received electric shock treatment. Her condition didn't improve until years later, when doctors discovered that lithium could control her mental imbalance.

A short time after Phil's family moved to Dixie, Pa fell eighteen feet from the floor of a drilling rig and landed on his head. He broke two vertebrae in his back and ruptured his stomach. The accident nearly killed him. Doctors fused the vertebrae in his back with bone from his hip and repaired his stomach. But Pa was forced to wear a heavy plaster of Paris cast from neck to hip for nearly two years and obviously couldn't work. Making matters worse, Granny was confined to the mental hospital at the same time, so Pa was left to care for five of his children while he was immobilized.

Phil's older brothers, Jimmy Frank and Harold, were

enrolled in classes at Louisiana State University in Baton Rouge. Both of them volunteered to come home and work to help the family make ends meet. But Pa insisted they stay in school and finish their education. The family somehow survived on Pa's disability checks of thirty-five dollars a week. Phil's older sister, Judy, did most of the cooking and cared for her younger siblings, Silas and Jan. Phil's other older brother Tommy and Phil gathered pecans and sold them to local markets. The family subsisted on rice and beans, cornbread, and whatever fish and game the boys could catch. Rice and beans was a staple dish at the Robertson dinner table. A hundred-pound bag of rice and several cans of beans would last for weeks. There are dozens of ways to prepare rice and beans, and the recipes could be altered by adding a simple gravy or squirrel, quail, or fish, so it was a perfect meal for the struggling Robertson family.

ABOUT THE ONLY THING PHIL CARED ABOUT OTHER THAN HUNTING AND FISHING WAS PLAYING FOOTBALL.

About the only thing Phil cared about other than hunting and fishing was playing football. The Robertson boys learned to play football in the backyard of their log home. They constructed a goalpost with oak-tree uprights and a gum-tree crossbar. Four of the Robertson boys played football at Vivian High School and later North Caddo High School (after the parish consolidated several schools). Jimmy Frank played center and guard but always wanted to be a quarterback. He taught his younger brothers how to play the position. Tommy was a track star and was the first Robertson to play quarterback, but moved to halfback when Phil made the varsity team at North Caddo High. Harold broke his elbow while playing on the freshman team and never played football again. Silas was a hard-hitting defensive back, but Phil ended up being the best athlete in the family. He was a first-team, all-state quarterback and all-district outfielder in baseball.

Phil and Kay started dating when she was in the ninth grade and he was in the tenth. She assisted the Robertson family at times by giving them food from the general store her family owned in Ida, Louisiana. Phil and Kay broke up during the Christmas holidays the year they started dating because Phil didn't want a girlfriend interfering with hunting season. But then Kay's father passed away the next May, and Phil attended his funeral. They started dating again soon thereafter.

After finishing high school, Phil received a football scholarship from Louisiana Tech University in Ruston, where his brother Tommy was already playing for the Bulldogs. Kay moved there with Phil and completed her senior year at Ruston High School. She was pregnant at the age of sixteen with my oldest brother, Alan. Phil and Kay moved into the same apartment complex where Tommy and his wife, the former Nancy Dennig, lived, which made the transition to college a lot easier. Phil was redshirted his freshman year at Louisiana Tech but then won the starting quarterback job the next season. He was ahead of Terry Bradshaw on the depth chart.

In his book *It's Only a Game*, Bradshaw remembered Phil: "He'd come out to practice directly from the woods, squirrel tails hanging out of his pockets, duck feathers on his clothes. Clearly he was a fine shot, so no one complained too much."

During one practice before his senior season, Phil saw a flock of geese fly over the practice field. Phil looked up at the geese and thought, "Man, what am I doing here?" He quit the football team a few days later, handing the starting job to Bradshaw. Bradshaw later led the NFL's Pittsburgh Steelers to four Super Bowl championships and was inducted into the Pro Football Hall of Fame in 1989. Phil stayed at Louisiana Tech and earned a bachelor's degree in health and physical education in 1969 and a master's in 1974. He spent the rest of his fall days in the bayou, hunting ducks and squirrels, instead of throwing touchdowns.

To be honest, I came along at a difficult time in Phil's life. After he earned his bachelor's degree at Louisiana Tech, he was hired to teach English and physical education at a school in Junction City, Arkansas. Phil spent most of his time fishing, hunting, and drinking with the guy who hired him. They were doing some pretty wild and crazy things, and Phil was reprimanded a few times by the school board for his boorish behavior. He quit his teaching job before they could fire him and signed an eighteen-month lease to run a honky-tonk at the bottom of the Ouachita River near El Dorado, Arkansas. Phil was drinking a lot and spending very little time with us. Kay was so worried about Phil that she began working as a barmaid at the honky-tonk to keep an eye on him.

TO BE HONEST, I CAME ALONG AT A DIFFICULT TIME IN PHIL'S LIFE.

When Phil and Kay were at the bar, they'd leave Alan, Jase, and me with Aunt Rose, who was my favorite babysitter. She wasn't actually our aunt, but in the South, when you're a kid you've got to put something in front of the name of any adult you talk to. It's a sign of respect, and having good manners is a big thing for us Southerners. Aunt Rose made clothes for us and took good care of us. I loved that woman.

There was another babysitter that I didn't have such warm feelings for. The only thing I remember about her is that she would always try to feed us Raisin Bran. Not that there is anything wrong with Raisin Bran, but I just happened to hate it. I would refuse to eat it, and she would lock me in the closet! Unfortunately for me, I spent a lot of time in the closet that summer. I'm not sure if Jase actually liked Raisin Bran or if seeing me locked in a closet was enough of a deterrent to make him eat it, but he seemed to be her favorite and immune to the closet torture. I'd complain to Kay and she would always say, "Why don't you just eat the Raisin Bran?" I guess I was stubborn even as a little kid.

There wasn't much Kay could do about it anyway; she was just trying to keep our family's head above the water. Phil's bar was nothing more than a low wooden building attached to a mobile home. He was the bartender and cook. He served fried chicken, pickled pig's feet, and boiled eggs. Occasionally, he'd cook venison or wild boar. But more than anything else, Phil just drank a lot. Phil's sister Jan was so concerned about his drinking that she brought a preacher, William "Bill" Smith, from White's Ferry Road Church in West Monroe, Louisiana, to his bar to try to save him. Phil took one look at the man and said, "Are you some kind of preacher?"

Smith said he was a preacher, and Phil asked him if he'd ever been drunk. Smith admitted he used to drink a few beers.

"Well, what's the difference between you and me?" Phil asked him. "You've been drunk and I'm getting drunk right now. You ain't putting the Bible on me."

Smith left the bar, and Phil went back to drinking.

One night, Phil was arguing with the bar's owner and his wife. He was drunk and threw the woman across the bar and beat both of them up pretty badly. When the police arrived to break up the melee, Phil slipped out the back door. Before he left, Phil told Kay she wouldn't see him for a while. Then he stayed in the woods for several weeks while the authorities were looking for him.

Phil left Kay behind to clean up the mess. The bar owners eventually agreed not to press charges against Phil, but Kay had to give them all the money they had earned while operating the bar. She was broke and unemployed. She moved our trailer to a spot close to D'Arbonne Lake near Farmerville, Louisiana. Kay got a job working in the corporate offices of Howard Brothers Discount Stores in Monroe, Louisiana, which, ironically, was owned by Korie's family. Our lives were beginning to intersect when we were just babies. God had a plan.

Kay was handling payroll and employee benefits. Phil finally came home and got a job working in the offshore oil fields in the Gulf of Mexico. Kay was happy our family was back together again.

During the time that Phil was working at the offshore drilling sites, Kay had to put us in a day-care facility while she worked. I was only three years old, but even then I was always trying to impress my friends. One day I decided to do something that had never been done before—climb up the slide backward. I shimmied my way up the slide while the other children oohed and ahhed. Once I got to the top, I turned to raise my hands in victory and to prove once and for all that I was king of the playground. I made a minor tactical error, however. That slide was slippery, and I fell eight feet to the ground right on top of a tree root. The teacher called my mom, who rushed me to St. Francis Medical Center, where they found I had shattered both of the bones in my thighs. One of the bones was splintered all the way from my knee to my hip.

I WAS ONLY THREE YEARS OLD, BUT EVEN THEN I WAS ALWAYS TRYING TO IMPRESS MY FRIENDS.

Being in the hospital was kind of fun because I got lots of attention and sympathy. What was not so exciting was the nearly full-body cast they had to put me in to keep me immobilized until the bones could fuse back together. They had to put me to sleep to insert a pin in my leg to hold the bone together. The cast completely covered my broken leg and went halfway down the other leg. It came all the way up to my chest, so I could not move at all from my waist down.

Word somehow got to Phil. I'm not sure how it happened since cell phones weren't invented then, and even if they were, Phil certainly would not have had one. At any rate, he found out and rushed home from his offshore job. He came to the hospital and started yelling at Kay for letting me break my leg, as if there was anything she could have done about it. At that point in my life, it didn't seem like Phil was really interested in us kids, but when I got hurt his concern was evident. He even spent the night in the hospital with me until I was allowed to go home. I don't know how he, Kay, and I all slept in that little hospital bed, but we did, and I felt loved and cared for, despite our somewhat nomadic existence up until this point in my life.

One of Phil's friends, Jerry Allen, owned a car dealership. Jerry brought me one of the roller seats that mechanics use to work on cars. I rolled around our trailer on the seat for three or four months, bumping into everything in the house. My aunts and uncles tell me they still remember me rolling around the seat in the yard, trying to keep up with my brothers and cousins. I must have looked like an ape trying to navigate the creeper with nothing but my arms! I remember that part being pretty fun, but my brothers just remember the smell. They say that cast stunk like crazy! You can imagine the smell after a summer in the Louisiana heat in a full-body cast. The doctors cut a hole out of the back, and Alan remembers having to carry me to the bathroom every time I had to go. It was rough. I probably should apologize to him for that one.

Also, I learned a difficult life lesson: sometimes in trying to be king of the playground, you could end up off the playground for about six months if you're not careful. In other words, as it says in the Bible: "Don't think of yourself [or climb] more highly than you ought, but rather think of yourself with sober judgment in accordance with the measure of faith God has given you" (Romans 12:3).

Things were okay for a while, but Phil was still drinking a lot, and one rainy night during a drinking binge, Phil told Kay he wanted her to take her sons and leave. He said he was sick and tired of all of us and wanted to live his own life. We spent the night at my uncle Harold's house, and then the church helped us get a low-rent apartment.

I was really too young to remember many of the details, but I know Kay was very worried that she was about to lose her husband and her sons were about to lose their father.

WILLIE'S BEANS AND RICE

You can be creative with this. Don't worry about doing it exactly the way it is written. If you don't have an ingredient, make it anyway. I make beans every time we make or buy a ham—the ham bone is the key. You will find hunks of that ham when it cooks off the bone that you never knew existed, and they are delicious. Never throw a ham bone away!

1 pound dry kidney or pinto beans

1 ham bone with as much ham left on it as you want (I buy one that is honey glazed, take the ham off for sandwiches, then use what's left for beans)

10 cups water, divided

⅓ cup olive oil, plus 1 teaspoon for frying

a couple of slices of bacon, cut up

1 large onion, diced

2 tablespoons minced garlic

1 green bell pepper, diced

2 stalks celery, diced

2 bay leaves (if you don't have any in your cabinet, don't worry about it)

½ teaspoon cayenne pepper (less if you are feeding kids)

1 tablespoon parsley flakes (again, don't sweat it if you don't have them)

1 teaspoon Phil Robertson's Cajun Style Seasoning

1 pound andouille sausage, sliced (add more if you like sausage, or a different kind if this is too spicy)

a pinch of brown sugar

2 cups long-grain white rice

Louisiana Hot Sauce

1. Rinse beans and transfer to a large pot with ham bone and 6 cups water. Make sure the water covers all the beans.
2. In a skillet, heat olive oil and cut-up bacon over medium heat. Sauté onion, garlic, bell pepper, and celery for 3 to 4 minutes.

3. Stir cooked vegetables into beans.
4. Season with bay leaves, cayenne pepper, parsley, and Cajun Style Seasoning.
5. Bring mixture to a boil and then reduce heat to medium and cook 4 to 6 hours, or until beans are tender. Check every 2 hours and add more water if needed.
6. Cut sausage into slices and brown in skillet on medium heat with a teaspoon of olive oil.
7. Stir sausage into beans toward the end of cooking time and continue to simmer for thirty minutes.
8. Add brown sugar to taste.
9. In a saucepan, bring 4 cups water and rice to a boil. Reduce heat, cover, and simmer for 20 minutes. Serve beans over steamed white rice and add plenty of Louisiana Hot Sauce.

2

FRIED BOLOGNA

THEREFORE, AS GOD'S CHOSEN PEOPLE, HOLY AND DEARLY
LOVED, CLOTHE YOURSELVES WITH COMPASSION, KINDNESS,
HUMILITY, GENTLENESS AND PATIENCE. BEAR WITH EACH OTHER
AND FORGIVE ONE ANOTHER IF ANY OF YOU HAS A GRIEVANCE
AGAINST SOMEONE. FORGIVE AS THE LORD FORGAVE YOU.
—COLOSSIANS 3:12–13

About three months after Phil kicked us out of the
house, Kay was working at Howard Brothers' corporate offices when one of her coworkers told her Phil
was sitting in his truck in the parking lot. Kay looked out the
window and saw Phil hunched over the steering wheel. She
figured he was probably drunk again. But when Kay got to his
truck, she found Phil crying. It was something she had never
seen before and probably has never seen since.

"I want my family back," Phil told her. "I'm so sorry."

Fortunately for all of us, Kay was strong enough to forgive
Phil and take him back. But she took him back with the following conditions: Phil had to quit drinking and walk away
from his rowdy friends. Kay enlisted the help of William
"Bill" Smith, the preacher at White's Ferry Road Church in

West Monroe, Louisiana, who Phil had run out of his bar several months earlier. In one of their early conversations, Smith asked Phil if he trusted him. Phil told him no, he didn't, so Smith held up a Bible.

"You don't have to trust me," Smith told him. "Trust what's written in here."

From that day forward, Phil started his study of God's Word. He attended church several times a week and started going to Bible study nearly every night. He was baptized at the age of twenty-eight and gave up drinking and partying altogether. We moved into an apartment on Pine Terrace in West Monroe in 1976. Kay rented the apartment under an assumed name and didn't give our address or phone number to any of Phil's friends. We shared the apartment with Granny and Pa, so seven of us (my youngest brother, Jep, wasn't born yet) were living in a two-bedroom apartment. It was pretty cramped, but we didn't care. The only thing that mattered was our family was back together again.

Alan, Jase, and I slept on the floor of the living room in army sleeping bags that my uncle Si had given us. Si had brought them back from Vietnam and they were stuffed with real goose feathers. I was only about four years old at the time and had a habit of wetting the bed nearly every night. Phil used to get onto me for peeing in the bed and would threaten to spank me every morning that my sleeping bag was wet. Like I could help it! I eventually figured out that I could hold my sleeping bag up to an old butane heater and dry it. I would pee in the bed and then wake up early so it would be dry before anybody else woke up. I can only imagine how bad that sleeping bag must have smelled! I doubt that I was fooling anyone. One of our kids was a bed wetter and I never disciplined that child for it. Bed-wetting was something I totally understood.

Phil took a job teaching at Ouachita Christian School, a new school in Ouachita Parish. He thought he needed to be around Christians as much as possible as he continued his spiritual healing. Phil still says the kids he taught at Ouachita Christian School influenced his Christian walk more than anyone else. They really left an impression on him at a time when he needed it most.

Kay kept working at the department store office, so my brothers and I spent a lot of time together. Alan was the oldest and was left in charge. He assumed the responsibility of caring for his younger brothers. He was a free babysitter for Phil and Kay more than anything else, as we still didn't have much money. Kay remembers some really rough times when Alan would feed Jase and me our bottles and put us to bed—he was only seven or eight years old himself.

KAY REMEMBERS SOME REALLY ROUGH TIMES WHEN ALAN WOULD FEED JASE AND ME OUR BOTTLES AND PUT US TO BED—HE WAS ONLY SEVEN OR EIGHT YEARS OLD HIMSELF.

My brothers and I really had a good time living in the apartment. I've always been a people person, and there were a lot of kids who lived in the complex. We would go out in the parking lot and do choreographed dances. This was the 1970s, so I guess we were being influenced by the movies of that time, which involved a lot of singing and dancing. *Saturday Night Fever, The Rocky Horror Picture Show,* and *Grease* were always some of our favorites.

Alan was in charge of feeding us lunch when Kay and Phil were at work. When it was just the kids, our standard meal was fried bologna sandwiches—they were cheap and easy to make. And for that reason, Mom always had a loaf of bologna in our icebox. We became bologna connoisseurs. Even though we were kids, we were still Robertsons, which meant we took our food very seriously. No ordinary bologna sandwiches with mayonnaise slapped between two slices of bread for us. I think we tried every way you could make bologna better. Our favorite way, which I still make from time to time today, involved cutting three slits in the bologna, creating three triangles that were held together by the middle. We did that so the bologna wouldn't bubble up too much while we were frying it. We would almost burn one side, then flip it and put a slice of cheese on the top while the other side was cooking. In the meantime, we would warm the bread in the pan so that it had a little flavor from the grease and was slightly toasted. Yum, I'm getting hungry thinking about it! A little cheese or butter on anything makes it better. All of our meals at that time involved at least one of those two items. Granny lived to ninety-six years old and Pa till eighty-seven, so I guess it wasn't all that bad.

WHEN IT WAS JUST THE KIDS, OUR STANDARD MEAL WAS FRIED BOLOGNA SANDWICHES.

The apartment got a little less cramped when Granny

and Pa moved to Arizona to work on the oil fields for a few months, but we didn't live there for long because soon Phil decided he could make more money as a commercial fisherman than a teacher and wanted to start working toward that goal. Being out in the woods or on the water was still what brought him the most joy. He told Kay to search for some land with access to water that eventually flowed into the Gulf of Mexico.

Kay searched the real estate listings in the newspapers and found an advertisement for a piece of property titled "Sportsman's Paradise." There were two houses on the land—which were really nothing more than fishing camps—and it came with six and a half acres. It was located just off the Ouachita River at the mouth of Cypress Creek. It was at the end of a dirt road in one of the most remote locations in the parish. When Kay took Phil to see the land, he knew instantly that it was where he wanted to live. Phil was convinced he could make a living fishing, and he wanted his sons to learn to hunt and fish and survive off the land like he had as a child. He believed our family could subsist on the fish and game we killed, along with fruits and vegetables we could grow in a garden. Phil wanted us to learn to become a man just like he had as a child growing up in the outdoors.

One of the houses was a white, two-bedroom frame house and the other was a smaller camp house that had green wooden siding. About the same time Kay and Phil were trying to buy the land, Pa and Granny were returning home from Arizona. Kay and Phil reached an agreement with my grandparents. Pa and Granny would provide the down payment for the property, and Phil and Kay would assume the monthly mortgage payments as my grandparents eased into retirement. Our family would live in the white house, and Pa and Granny would live in the green one.

I still remember the day Phil and Kay took us to see our new home for the first time. It is one of the happiest memories from my childhood. We pulled to the end of the dirt road and all the kids jumped out of the car and ran to the house. It was like heaven to us. Woods surrounded the house, which sat on stilts at the top of a hill to avoid flooding from the river. You could see the Ouachita River from the front porch. Phil and Kay still live in the same house today. I don't think there's anything that could convince them to leave that house. It is home.

After we moved into the house, Alan and Jase started school again. I was still too young to attend, so I spent most of my time with my granny and pa. Phil worked at the school for that first year while he got his commercial fishing business going and Kay continued to work at Howard Brothers Discount Stores.

This was a fun time in my life, with great memories of spending time with Granny and Pa. I had them all to myself while Jase and Alan were in school. I would sit at the table with them and play cards and dominoes, and we watched a lot of TV even though we only had three channels. We watched *The Price Is Right* in the morning and soap operas like *All My Children* and *As the World Turns* in the afternoon. When Granny was eighty, she actually appeared on *The Price Is Right* and won the game! It was "Spring Break Week," and she competed against a bunch of college-aged kids. Granny was really good with numbers. Bob Barker would ask her the price of an item and she'd immediately yell out, "Six dollars, Bob!" Most of the college kids on the show didn't know anything and were looking to the crowd for help, but Granny knew the price of everything almost immediately. She won two cars and a trip to Fort Lauderdale, Florida, on the Showcase Showdown.

Granny was very opinionated and fun to be around. She would take me places, like the county fair or into town. She even let me burn things—which I loved. This was not a weird pyromaniac thing. When you live in the country, burning things is a way of life. There is no trash man who comes to pick up your trash. You just make a pile and burn it. I was barely five years old, at the time, but I made a deal with Granny that I would clean up her yard if she would let me burn the pile. Every day, I'd go out in the yard and rake up piles of leaves and sticks and set them on fire. I burned everything. I just loved building fires, and—you can ask Korie—I still do. We've had the fire department visit us a few times when they have had reports that a fire I started

I MADE A DEAL WITH GRANNY THAT I WOULD CLEAN UP HER YARD IF SHE WOULD LET ME BURN THE PILE.

was out of control, but I'm proud to say that they've never had to actually put one out. I always had the fire under control by the time they arrived.

I'd help Granny in the garden, too. One time I pulled the stem out of a cantaloupe because I thought that's what I was supposed to do. Pa thumped me upside the head for doing it, and then Granny slapped him upside the head for hitting me. All of my cousins believed I was Granny's favorite because I spent so much time with her.

Granny was still having mental problems at the time, but I was too young to understand what was going on. She would do some really odd things. We had a chicken coop, and sometimes she would sit out there and crow with the chickens. Sometimes she would have her clothes on and sometimes she wouldn't. One day I was walking on the concrete sidewalk between our houses, and Granny kicked open the screen door on the front of her house. She had a rifle and shot out a string of lights hanging between the trees. I guess that's where my dad got his shooting skills. She was a heck of a shot.

One time Granny had a bunch of bananas and started peeling them and cleaning her windows with them. Before she went to the hospital for an extended stay, she went through her house and painted everything that was a rectangle with red paint. She even painted her Bible red! When Granny came back from the hospital, she couldn't figure out who painted everything in her house red. She didn't even know she had done it.

Being young, I didn't know anything was wrong with her. I just thought all the eccentric things she did were normal. That was just how she was. I was a bit of an entrepreneur, though, and took advantage of her generosity. She owned a small boat dock at the mouth of Cypress Creek and people would leave a dollar every time they used the dock. Because of that dock, Granny always had a pocket full of money. I'd take her garbage out and she'd pay me like $120 without even realizing it. She even paid me to throw away Pa's stuff one time when she was mad at him. I threw a bunch of his tools in the river. I still feel kind of bad about that one, but I was just a little kid. I didn't know any better, plus she had a pocket full of green bills calling my name.

Pa was the quietest man I've ever known. He would sit at the table playing solitaire with a cigarette hanging out of his mouth. They both smoked like freight trains. I can't believe I don't have lung cancer from spending so much time with them. I was definitely exposed to some serious secondhand smoke. Pa would be playing cards, and Granny would want to get his attention, so she would walk by the table and grab a handful of his cards and throw them in the fireplace. Pa would look at her and just say, "Aw, crap," and then start watching TV as if nothing had happened.

Like Phil and Kay, our granny and pa taught us how to be independent, confident, and self-sufficient. They raised seven great kids, my dad and aunts and uncles, and made it through some really tough times together. I loved both of them dearly and am thankful for the time I got to spend with them. I think there is something really special about spending time with people from their generation. It's called the Greatest Generation for a reason. They knew how to make the best of what they had—even if it was just fried bologna.

FRIED BOLOGNA SANDWICHES

If you are worried about grease or butter, then you probably should not eat this. I have to admit, I don't eat them much anymore, but when I do, it takes me back in time.

1 tablespoon butter
2 slices thick-cut bologna
bacon grease if you have it (Granny always saved her bacon
    grease to cook with)
2 slices bread
2 slices of any type of cheese

1. Melt butter in frying pan.
2. Cut three slits in each slice of bologna and fry in butter. Add cheese. Remove from pan when done.
3. Warm bacon grease in frying pan.
4. Toast slices of bread in hot bacon grease.
5. Place bologna and cheese between slices of bread.

FRIED CATFISH

BUT AS FOR ME AND MY HOUSEHOLD, WE WILL SERVE THE LORD.
—JOSHUA 24:15

Korie: "More fish, Papaw! More fish!"

My papaw Howard loved to hear me say those words. We would catch fish together almost every day, then would go straight inside and fry them up. I loved eating fish; I even ate the tails. Most important, I loved spending time with Papaw. My brother, Ryan, was always shooting squirrels with his BB gun, and I remember Papaw teaching me how to skin one of the squirrels that Ryan killed.

Other than that, I guess Phil would call my family yuppies. Living in West Monroe, Louisiana, you can't be too much of a city girl, though. It's a pretty small town, where most people enjoy hunting and fishing to some extent. But I did live in a subdivision and attended a private school, and the only time I remember my dad going hunting was on a business trip with some of his big clients. So I guess that qualifies us as yuppies.

Alton Howard, my papaw, was semiretired at fifty-three

years old. So while he lived in a big, beautiful house in a sub-division, he had time to teach us a thing or two about country living. Papaw grew up in Rocky Branch, Louisiana, in an environment much like the one Phil grew up in. Papaw always told us stories of feeding the hogs and getting oranges in his stocking for Christmas. His family worked hard to survive, and he learned how to live off the land. Papaw served four years in the Army Air Forces during World War II. Then Papaw came home, where he met my beautiful mamaw, Mamie Jean, in a bowling alley in West Monroe. They married and set out to make their fortune. Partnering with one of his brothers, Papaw opened a jewelry store, where I remember "working" as a young girl. I enjoyed going to the store and helping clean the glass counters and wrap the gifts at Christmastime. They had a machine that made bows, and I especially loved making them. The jewelry store was just the beginning, though. Papaw and my father, Johnny, were involved in more than twenty business ventures together, including a chain of stores called Howard Brothers Discount Stores (this is the company Kay worked for when she and the boys first came to West Monroe).

The discount stores opened their doors in 1959 as a Gibson's franchise. This was a few years before Wal-Mart opened. The company went public in 1969 and changed its name from Gibson's to Howard Brothers Discount Stores, which became a very successful chain, with seventy-eight stores all over the Southeast. My dad finished college and went straight to work for the family businesses. So Duck

Commander's being a family business was nothing unusual for me. I was very familiar with the unique benefits and challenges that come with a family-run operation. My mamaw Howard loved to cook for her family, and we lived just across the pond from them so we ate at their house quite a bit. Mamaw was and still is a great woman of God. She's always reading Bible verses to us and is living proof that the prayers of the righteous are powerful and effective. My papaw loved her dearly and called her "Queenie." She would set the table, and my dad and papaw would sit down to eat and talk over their latest business deals. I loved to listen in.

The discount stores were sold in 1978, but my father continued to work for the company for five years and then went on to other business adventures. He visited a Price Club store, the forerunner of Costco, on a trip to California and came back and told my papaw, "Here's something Sam Walton will never do!" The Wal-Mart stores had grown exponentially during those years, and the last thing they wanted to do was be in competition with Sam Walton. And so my papaw and father started SuperSaver Wholesale Warehouse Club in 1984. They didn't realize that about that same time Sam Walton was opening new stores called Sam's Club. SuperSaver grew fast, with twenty-four stores opening in only eighteen months! Papaw and Daddy were about to take the company public when Sam Walton called with an offer. Sam bought SuperSaver from my family in 1987 and those twenty-four stores became Sam's Clubs. So needless to say, I came from a very business-minded family! It's what they loved to do. For the Robertsons, the motto has always been faith, family, and ducks. But for my side of the family it's more like Faith, Family, and Business!

I had a great upbringing. I came from strong Christian families on both sides and was blessed to always have the security of a mom and dad who loved God, loved each other, and took care of our needs. My mamaw and papaw on my mom's side, Jo and Luther Shackelford, met in San Diego, California, where my papaw served in the marines during the Korean War. He was recruited to play basketball for the marines, and my mamaw was a cheerleader. Papaw Shack was six feet four inches, and a strong legacy of basketball players continues to this day in our family because of him. He went to college on the GI Bill and earned a master's degree in engineering from Oklahoma State University. He and my mamaw lived in Shreveport, Louisiana, for most of my childhood, which is only about an hour and a half from West Monroe, where I grew up, and I loved going to visit them. When I was young, I called them Mamaw and Papaw Shreveport!

When I went to visit, Mamaw would have the fridge stocked with all of my favorite things, and Papaw always had a joke to tell and a hug and a kiss for me. He was the kindest man I have ever known, with a word of encouragement always on his lips. My papaw was a salesman for most of his life. Mamaw always said he could "sell a refrigerator to an Eskimo." Mamaw was a busy stay-at-home mom with six kids. She could do absolutely anything and still can. She doesn't look like your typical grandma. And at eighty, if she doesn't yet, I don't think she ever will! She's always stylish and up for the next adventure. She is truly a product of the Greatest Generation, with the ability to sew all her kids' clothes and cook fantastic meals, and even, as my mom tells us, once enclosed their garage to make a game room and laid the brick all by herself! She started working with my Papaw in real estate after her kids were grown and is still working today. She's running their real estate office and serving on the board of the Northeast Louisiana Association of Realtors, along with keeping up with her grandkids and great-grandkids.

My parents, John and Chrys Howard, met at Camp Ch-Yo-Ca (the same camp where Willie and I met) and were married a few years later when my mom was eighteen years old. They headed off to Harding University, and I was born two years later on October 24, 1973. When we go back to Searcy, Arkansas, where the Harding campus is, my dad loves to point out where I was conceived, in a trailer between a meatpacking plant and a graveyard. Awkward!

Now back to my parents' meeting at camp. Camp Ch-Yo-Ca, which stands for CHristian YOuth CAmp, was started in 1967 by my mamaw and papaw Howard, along with several other men and women. They had a dream of having a place for kids and teens to get out of their normal environment, spend time in the woods, have fun with friends, and, most important, grow closer to God. Growing up, my mom, along with my brother, Ryan, and sister, Ashley, and I, lived out there every summer in an RV parked in front of the craft shed. The camp was only about ten minutes from our house, but it is set in the middle of one hundred acres, and when we were there, we felt like we were in the middle of nowhere. My dad would come in and out because he still had to work, of course. He was busy growing the family business.

Some of my favorite memories are of being at camp. We spent the entire summer outdoors. There were no televisions, just Ping-Pong tables, swings, a lake for fishing and canoeing, and a giant swimming pool. Since we were the "camp kids," we were there for every session, and we loved it. We roamed free and played all day. We would sneak into the kitchen and go into the walk-in refrigerator to cool off. It's hot in Louisiana in the summertime! I was kind of shy as a child, so one summer when I was about nine, everybody's favorite camp director, Howard Karbo, decided I was not getting near enough attention. He started the "Korie Howard Fan Club." This fan club didn't exactly do anything, and I think there were only about two members. While I was a little embarrassed by the attention, what girl wouldn't be flattered to have her own fan club?

My mom taught the crafts and later went on to be a director at the camp, and still is today. My mom has more energy than any woman I know. She works so hard for those kids. She has a servant spirit like none other. She has worked most of her life as a volunteer in some capacity, whether at the camp or at the Christian school that we attended. She started a program at our school for kids with learning difficulties and worked there every day for twelve years, never taking a paycheck.

By that time, my family had launched a publishing company called Howard Publishing, which was later sold to Simon & Schuster, and she was needed there. She eventually went on to work as a senior editor and creative director for the company. Mom was the kind of mother who loved to make things fun for everybody. She was the one who planned the class parties, and the youth group at our church always hung out at my family's house. They still do to this day. Mom brought all of that fun to the publishing company, having monthly lunches to honor the employees and a month of activities at Christmastime, including Pancake and Pajama Day. (I've thought of doing that at Duck Commander, but I'm not sure if I could talk the guys into coming to work in their PJs. Actually, the thought of that is a little scary!) Her work in this area helped the company win the "Best Christian Workplace in America" award for five years in a row!

Mom continues to make life fun for her grandkids. They call her Two-Mama and call my dad Two-Papa, and we couldn't live without them! We built a house next door to my parents about five years ago, and our kids just go back and forth. It's been an extra blessing while we're filming the show. Life's busy, and I never feel guilty about leaving my kids with Two-Mama while I film or work. Two-Mama is always there, and I know they're in great hands!

Some of my other favorite memories of growing up are of us traveling as a family. I think traveling is a great gift to be able to give your kids in order to expose them to different cultures and people around the world. My dad always took time off to take us on awesome vacations. We went snow skiing every winter and to the beach every summer. We were blessed to be able to go incredible places like China, Austria, and Germany, and we even went to two Olympic Games. Not all of the places we traveled were that exotic though. Every year, we went with Mamaw and Papaw Howard on what we called "Grandkids' Vacation." My papaw Howard had an RV, so this was usually a road trip to Branson, Missouri. One year the RV broke down right in front of a mall. Papaw said that was his most expensive breakdown ever. We shopped the whole time we waited for the RV to get fixed!

Like I said, Dad was a hard worker. He didn't golf, hunt, or have any other hobbies besides work and family. He never missed any of our sporting events, and nowadays, he never misses one of the grandkids' activities. He may be in the stands reading over a contract, but he is there. He's a great Two-Papa. One time our daughter, Bella, was telling me how Two-Papa's favorite thing to do is to take them anywhere they want to go. All the grandkids know that if they want something, ask Two-Papa. Every time they ask him to take them on a snow cone run, he stops whatever he's doing and says, "I was waiting for you to ask me that!" And they hop in his T-Bird and go get snow cones. The best thing about it is that he not only takes them, but he makes them feel like that's exactly what he wanted to do.

After Dad sold Howard Publishing to Simon & Schuster, he continued as the president of the company for three years. Then after he and Mom took some time off to travel,

Daddy came to work for us at Duck Commander, working with budgets and contracts. You know we like to keep it all in the family! He is an invaluable asset with all of his business knowledge and experience. Plus, Dad's a detail person, while Willie is more of a big-picture guy. Like everything else at Duck Commander, it seems that when Dad came on board, God provided us with what we needed most, and He continues to do it over and over again.

Yep, there are a lot of differences between our two families. Unlike Kay, Mom is not a cook. She actually doesn't even care about food. Never has. I would say Mom pretty much just eats to live rather than lives to eat like the Robertson family. Dad had colon cancer in 2000, and my parents became pescetarians after that, which means they eat only fruit, veggies, and things that swim. They actually went to a "camp" to learn how to eat vegetarian. We've made fun of them for years for going to "veggie camp," but I have actually tried to get Willie to go there with me sometime. I don't want to give up meat, but it wouldn't hurt to get more veggies in our diet. I doubt I'll ever get him to set foot there, but he did actually get into juicing recently. We are using my parents' juicer until we make sure it sticks. He's loving it; he says it's fun creating new juicing "recipes," and they actually don't taste that bad! So while my mom is no Miss Kay in the kitchen, there are things we can learn from both sides of the family in regards to food.

It's pretty plain to see the differences in our families, but what you may not realize is that they are alike in the most critical way—our faith. Some of the most important lessons my parents taught me were those of generosity and service. I really can't remember a time when we didn't have someone living in our home who needed a place to stay—from struggling single moms with kids to entire families that needed somewhere to live while they got back on their feet. I saw this same trait in the Robertson family, and I loved it. They may not have had as much as we did growing up, but the generosity of spirit and hospitality was there just the same. Their home was always open, and there was always an extra spot at the dinner table for whoever needed a helping hand or just someone to talk to. As it says in Psalm 41:1–2: "Blessed are those who have regard for the weak; the Lord delivers them in times of trouble. The Lord protects and preserves them—they are counted among the blessed in the land—He does not give them over to the desire of their foes."

My family has been very successful in business, but none of that would have mattered without our faith in God. While we were growing up, my parents would often tell us that all the blessings we had were nice, but if we lost it all tomorrow, we would still be just fine. And I always believed it. I think that is one of the reasons Willie and I were willing to take the risks we needed to with Duck Commander. We always had the faith that if we failed, if we lost it all, we would just shake ourselves off and get right back up. As long as we had our faith and our family, nothing could really hurt us. God has blessed us, life is good, but if the fame and fortune that we've enjoyed through Duck Commander were all gone tomorrow, I would still say the same thing: that God is good.

FRIED CATFISH

Go catch 'em! It's hard to mess up this recipe. Be patient and wait on the grease; make sure it is hot. When the catfish come out, you only have a few seconds to "hit" them with seasoning. Cut the dark parts out of the fish; they taste terrible.

peanut oil (enough to fill pot to about 4 inches deep)
8 catfish fillets, skin removed
1 tablespoon salt
2 tablespoons pepper
Phil Robertson's Cajun Style Seasoning, to taste
3 cups cornmeal

1. Heat a fryer or a deep pot halfway filled with oil to 350 degrees.
2. Sprinkle both sides of each catfish fillet with salt, pepper, and Cajun Style Seasoning.
3. Coat fish with cornmeal.
4. Place fillets in fryer and deep-fry for approximately 7 to 8 minutes until well-done.
5. Set catfish on paper towels and add one more sprinkle of Cajun Style Seasoning.

4

FREE LUNCH

I still remember my first day of school. Kay put me on the school bus and waved good-bye.

Korie: Willie rode the school bus on his very first day of kindergarten! And he wasn't even scarred for life! I'm kidding, of course, but this did shock me when I first heard it. It was so different from my experience. At our house, the first day of school was a big deal every year, not just kindergarten. Mom would take pictures of us in our "first day" outfits, drive us there, go in and meet the teacher, and make sure we had all of our supplies.

Today, we make a big deal out of the first day of school in

our home as well. We got together with my mom on the first day for a prayer before the kids start the new school year, asking God to bless them and to allow them to be a light for Him to their friends throughout the school year. We've been doing that ever since John Luke started his first day of kindergarten. He doesn't let me take his picture with his teachers anymore, but I still take whatever pictures I can. I, at least, make him take one picture with his brother and sisters on the first day of school and he appeases me, because I'm his mom, and he loves me!

I can just imagine little Willie getting on that school bus for his first day all by himself, full of confidence and certain that if he just flashed those dimples, the world would be his. And it usually was.

Somehow I made it to Pinecrest Elementary School and jumped off the bus with my little book satchel. The principal was standing there when I got off the bus.

"Hey, I'm Willie Jess Robertson and I'm looking for the kindergarten room," I told him in the most professional way I could.

The principal pointed down a hall and said, "It's right down there."

I got to my teacher's room and one of my best friends, Mel Hamilton, was crying because I wasn't there yet. I consoled him and was proud that someone needed me. School was going to be fun.

When I started kindergarten, we received free lunches

because our family didn't have any money. I thought everybody was on free lunch; I didn't even realize we were poor. But there were actually only about three kids in my class receiving free lunches, and I was one of them. There was a little boy who sat in front of me in kindergarten, and I thought he was really poor. He would come to school covered in dirt and didn't smell very good. One day, I took a bar of soap to school and put it on his desk. I wasn't trying to be mean or anything; I just didn't think he had any soap at home. Later in life, once I realized that we were getting the free lunches because we were poor just like that little kid, I remember thinking, "Man, were we that poor?"

> I THOUGHT EVERYBODY WAS ON FREE LUNCH; I DIDN'T EVEN REALIZE WE WERE POOR.

Over the next few years, I noticed that our family was beginning to make more money. When we went from receiving free lunches to getting reduced lunches, I thought that was a sign that Duck Commander was taking off. When we started paying for our own lunches, I thought, "Man, we must be rich now!"

The Robertson boys had a good reputation at school. Phil and Kay made sure that we treated our classmates and teachers with respect. They always insisted we behave at school and listen to our teachers. Even if we weren't the best-dressed students and didn't even have enough money to pay for our lunches, we were all voted class favorite at one time or another. Actually, I was voted "class favorite" several years in elementary school and was class president in ninth grade, with the campaign slogan "Don't be silly, vote for Willie!"

I learned how to make extra money at an early age. I thought I was the cutest kid in school, so I was surely going to use it to my advantage. In elementary school, the concession stand never sold the candy I liked to eat, so I decided I was going to bring my own candy to school and sell it to my classmates. It started with a box of chewing gum someone had given us. I took the gum to school and sold it for thirty cents apiece. Then I had Kay take me to the store, and I bought Lemon Heads, Red Hots, Mike and Ikes, and all sorts of other candy. I stored the candy in my locker, and my classmates started calling me the "Little Tycoon." I was making like three hundred dollars a week, minus the 10 percent I paid Kay for driving me to the store for supplies.

Now, there were some occupational hazards associated with the job. Darla Leonard, who rode my school bus, was older than me. She would strong-arm me every morning and make me give her free candy.

"No, it's thirty cents," I would tell her.

"How about nothing?" Darla would say before grabbing a fistful of my hair.

It made me so mad, but she was bigger than me, so there wasn't much I could do about it. She goes to our church now, and I could definitely take her these days. She's a tiny little woman, so it's funny to think that I was once scared of her.

After a few months of selling the candy, the principal called me to his office.

"I'm hearing you're selling candy to other students," Mr. McCall told me. "Are you?"

There was no denying it.

"The concession stand's sales are way down and they're complaining about it," the principal said. "I'm going to have to shut you down."

I quit selling the candy, but I still found other ways to make money. I sold everything from pencils and erasers to orange juice tops (which I claimed once sat on Abraham Lincoln's eyes!). The kids were just used to giving me their money, so I found creative ways to take it. I would eat June bugs for fifty cents and sing on the school bus for a quarter. One of my favorite moneymaking schemes involved my turning into a human jukebox. Kids would put quarters under my arms, and I would start singing. The only songs I knew were the ones my older brother Alan had on eight-tracks. Foreigner's "Juke Box Hero" was always the number one request, but I also sang songs by the Beach Boys, the Gap Band, Molly Hatchet, and Michael Jackson. I was the school bus entertainment. We went to a small country school so everyone lived far apart. I think we were on the bus about two hours each way, so this was a great way to pass the time.

I WOULD EAT JUNE BUGS FOR FIFTY CENTS AND SING ON THE SCHOOL BUS FOR A QUARTER.

Phil's philosophy about education was a lot like his philosophies about everything else in life. If my brothers or I told Phil we wanted to quit high school, he would look at us and say, "You wanna drop out of school? Knock yourself out, but don't come running to me." Then Phil would tell us that he wouldn't recommend quitting school. He would always tell us to make the best grades we could make, get our homework done, earn our diplomas, and get out of there. I've heard people talk about "helicopter parenting," where the parents hover over their kids, watching their every move. There was no danger of that in our house. We were pretty much on our own and were expected to do the best we could do with it.

Phil never told us we had to go to college or anything like that. If we woke up in the morning and decided we wanted to blow off school, we would just blow it off. Phil would never say anything about it. I never asked for Phil's permission to stay home; if I didn't want to go to school, I just didn't go. But Phil always told me if I missed too many days and got kicked out of school, I would have to deal with the consequences. We missed the maximum amount of days you could possibly miss every year, mainly during hunting season. We took full advantage of sick days to spend time in the woods.

Korie: This was not the case in my house. If you stayed home from school, you were going to the doctor, so you had to weigh the pros and cons. We took school seriously. We were never punished for making bad grades or anything like that; it was just expected that we'd work hard in school and do the best we could. And we did. Mom would say that school and the after-school activities we were involved in were our "job," and we were expected to give it our all. If we started something, we couldn't just quit it because we didn't want to do it anymore. We had to finish what we started. If it was a sport, we were part of a team and had a responsibility to our teammates to give it our best.

Mom was big on our learning new skills, so I took everything from tennis to baton lessons, diving to piano lessons, and played every sport at least one year. I think it gave me confidence that I could do anything if I worked at it. I still impress my kids with my backflips off the diving board and gymnastic tricks on the trampoline, but the piano lessons never stuck. The best I can do today is "Chopsticks," and I took piano for three years! I just wasn't good at it. My brother, on the other hand, plays piano beautifully.

> MOM WOULD SAY THAT SCHOOL AND THE AFTER-SCHOOL ACTIVITIES WE WERE INVOLVED IN WERE OUR "JOB," AND WE WERE EXPECTED TO GIVE IT OUR ALL.

With our children, I try to find the happy middle ground between how I was raised and Willie's upbringing. We expect our kids to do well in school and they all do, but there are times when we just decide to stay home. I figure the school gives us fifteen days a year for a reason. We might as well take them. Also, I want our kids to learn several different skills so they can find the thing they are good at and that they love, but I don't sign them up for quite as much as we did when I was a kid. I remember feeling like we were always on the go and just wanted to be home more at times. So I make sure our kids are involved in at least one sport, but the other lessons we try to space out so we don't spend our afternoons in the car rushing from one event to the next. I like for them to have the time to just be home and to explore and sometimes even to be bored and learn to create their own adventures.

When I was growing up in West Monroe, you technically didn't start high school until you were in the tenth grade. The ninth grade was still considered a part of middle school back then. We attended a middle school out in the country, but then everybody moved up to West Monroe High School in the tenth grade. When I was getting ready to go to the tenth grade in 1987, though, they were in the process of building a new high school. All of the kids from my part of the parish were allowed to choose whether they wanted to start the school year at West Monroe or go to the new school that was called West Ouachita.

Well, I decided to try out the new school since it was closer to home, and it seemed like the best choice. I went to the first day of school and checked in. I went to PE class on the first day, but we couldn't play basketball because they still hadn't put up the lights in the gymnasium. We had to sit there for an hour doing nothing. After about three days of sitting there, I said, "Screw this. I'm going to West Monroe High." I realized I wanted to be in town anyway, so I just transferred schools during the first week of school.

After about a month, the principal from West Ouachita called our house.

"Willie hasn't been to school for twenty-seven days," the principal told Phil.

"Well, he leaves for school every morning," Phil told him. "I don't know where he's going. I thought he was going to school."

"WILLIE HASN'T BEEN TO SCHOOL FOR TWENTY-SEVEN DAYS," THE PRINCIPAL TOLD PHIL.

When I got home that day, Phil asked me where I had been.

"School," I told him.

"Uh-uh," Phil said. "The school called and said you haven't been there in a month."

"Oh, yeah," I told him. "I transferred to West Monroe. I don't go to that school anymore."

"Okay," Phil said. "I figured something was up."

Korie: Can you imagine a tenth-grader transferring schools without even notifying his parents? Willie just showed up at West Monroe High School and said, "Hey, I'm here." He didn't even think about telling Kay and Phil about transferring.

When I got to high school, like most teens, I was becoming more and more social, so my entire objective was to get to town and stay there. Phil and Kay lived way out on the Ouachita River (they still live there today), and it's about a twenty-minute drive into town. Once I went to town, I knew I wasn't going home for a few days, because Phil and Kay never made a special trip to pick us up.

We lived so far out of town that I rarely spent the night at home during the week during my high school years. I spent a lot of nights with my best friend, Paul Lewis, who is African-

American, and his dad would cook all this weird stuff. I ate possum for the first time at Paul's house. I started eating the meat on my plate, and I was like, "Oh, my goodness." It had these tiny little legs. Paul's daddy had shot a possum and just threw it on the grill. It was nasty. Paul's daddy would also cook turtles and raccoons. You could bring him just about anything you killed, and he would cook it.

I was running around town with Paul all the time. I think it's safe to say I was the only white kid in his neighborhood. We were shooting basketball on the square one day, and a cop drove by and called me over to his police car. The cop asked me, "What are you doing over here? You don't need to be in this neighborhood."

"I know everybody in this neighborhood," I told him. "I practically live here."

Korie: By the time Willie was in high school, his parents pretty much just let him do his own thing. Willie slept wherever he could find a bed and meal. He even stayed at our house sometimes, which was fun. We were just friends at the time, so my parents didn't have a problem with it. He'd stay with Paul and with Mike Kellett, our youth minister, quite a bit too. Because Willie's parents' house was so far out of town, he and his brothers fended for themselves and were really, really independent. Willie didn't get his driver's license till he was seventeen years old just because nobody took him. He never told us he didn't have his license, though, and would drive my mom's van sometimes when he stayed at our house.

She didn't find out till we were married that he didn't have his license when he was driving her car. My dad about died!

Even though Kay and Phil let us run around town in middle school and high school, I don't think it was neglect or anything like that. Phil just never let anyone tell him what to do or how to do it, so I guess he figured we'd be the same way. He doesn't believe in going by what the world says you "should" do to have a good life or to be successful. Phil's philosophy was pretty simple: just follow what the Bible says and you'll be all right. And for the most part, we did.

I think my life was also shaped in a big way by what Kay and Phil and Pa and Granny taught each of us at an early age: be content with what you have and don't worry about what you don't have. Even in the lean times, there was a lot of

> PHIL'S PHILOSOPHY WAS PRETTY SIMPLE: JUST FOLLOW WHAT THE BIBLE SAYS AND YOU'LL BE ALL RIGHT. AND FOR THE MOST PART, WE DID.

love and laughter in the house. Some of my best memories are from when we had nothing. Who says you can't live on love? I think we did. We were thankful for what we had, comfortable with who we were, and always confident. We were Robertsons, for goodness' sake! And that meant something. When I was younger, I never believed I was different from anyone else—even if we were receiving free lunches.

WILLIE'S MEATLOAF

Be creative on this one. I got my foundation for this out of The Joy of Cooking *(which I go to all the time), then I started making stuff up. My only note on this: If the meat is full of grease, drain it. Check the meat while it is cooking. It's tricky to drain but do it if you have to. Growing up I hated meatloaf, but this one I like.*

2 pounds ground beef
1 pound andouille sausage
2 cups white onion, diced
1 clove garlic, minced
1½ cups bread crumbs, divided
⅔ cup parsley flakes
1 teaspoon oregano
1 teaspoon thyme
2 cups ketchup, divided
1 15-ounce can tomato sauce
4 eggs, beaten
2 cups mozzarella cheese
1 cup Parmesan cheese
1 tablespoon Phil Robertson's Cajun Style Seasoning
1 teaspoon salt
1 teaspoon pepper
5 or 6 slices bacon

1. Preheat oven to 350 degrees.
2. In a large cast-iron pot, combine ground beef, sausage, onion, garlic, 1 to 1¼ cups bread crumbs, parsley, oregano, thyme, 1 cup ketchup, tomato sauce, eggs, and mozzarella cheese. Use hands to thoroughly mix together.
3. Smooth meat mix in bottom of pot.
4. Cover meatloaf with Parmesan cheese, remaining bread crumbs, Cajun Style Seasoning, salt, and pepper.
5. Top meatloaf with remaining cup of ketchup and bacon.
6. Cook for 1½ hours, until middle of meatloaf is no longer pink.

5

TOAST 'N' PIZZA

A FRIEND LOVES AT ALL TIMES, AND A BROTHER
IS BORN FOR A TIME OF ADVERSITY.
—PROVERBS 17:17

When you watch *Duck Dynasty,* it might be pretty easy to see that Jase and I are very competitive. When we were younger, whether it was fishing, hunting, playing sports, or just about anything else, Jase and I loved a good competition. It wasn't just against each other. We would challenge anybody, but since we were the closest in age and lived all the way down at the mouth of the river, a long drive from civilization, for the most part we were all we had. So competing against each other and, more important, beating each other (and then reminding the loser about the details of our victory afterward) became our favorite pastime. It was that way when we were kids, and it's still that way today—whether it's in business, duck hunting, fishing, or golf.

When we were younger, we would spend every weekend and summer day competing against each other in something. Every day was about who could catch the most fish, throw the football the farthest, or shoot the most squirrels. When we wanted to go fishing, Phil and Kay would never buy bait for us, so we would have to go out and find our own bait. I was really good at it. We'd catch crickets or grasshoppers or dig for earthworms. Our neighbors had some catalpa trees and they were always covered with black worms that had two lines on their backs. We would take those worms and just go wear fish out with them. I used those worms in one of my earliest business ventures. I set up an old boat and literally filled it with cow manure. Our neighbors had cows, so I spent days picking it up to get an entire boatful. I would just pick it up with my hands. Worms thrive in cow manure, so I created a worm farm in it, and these worms were huge! Remember the boat dock that Granny charged people to use? Well, it was an easy marketplace. My customers were coming to me. I would set up my little stand and sell worms for five cents apiece all day long. Nowadays, Korie's always asking me to go buy bait for the kids when they want to go fishing. Now, I can afford it, but something seems wrong about buying something you can find for yourself if you'll just go outside and turn over a few logs.

I carried my fishing pole with me everywhere. We would fish on Cypress Creek, which ran next to our house, as well as sneak on other people's ponds to fish. As Jase and I got older, we started expanding our fishing territory. Judge John Harrison, the state district judge in Monroe, had a fishing camp up the road from our house. The judge was only there on the weekends, so we'd sneak under his gate and fish his pond all week when he wasn't around. The judge had built a bridge across his pond, and the first time I saw it, I was like, "You've got to be kidding me!" I was so excited my arms were actually shaking while I held my fishing pole off the bridge. I threw my line into the pond and a fish immediately hit the hook. My cork flew under the water, and I immediately dropped my pole. I ran back to our house as fast as I could to get Jase.

THE JUDGE WAS ONLY THERE ON THE WEEKENDS, SO WE'D SNEAK UNDER HIS GATE AND FISH HIS POND ALL WEEK WHEN HE WASN'T AROUND.

"I've found the mother lode!" I told Jase. "You will not believe how many fish are in this pond!"

Jase and I ran back to the judge's pond, and we stayed there the entire summer. We probably caught every bream in the pond and then we put out trout lines. We even carried our boat up the river and into the pond and fished from it all summer. When we were done fishing for the day, we would leave our poles behind and hide the boat. One time when we came back, the judge had taken our fishing poles, so we knew he was onto us, but that didn't stop us. By the end of the summer, we had cut a ditch under the gate from sliding under it. When we were finished with that pond, you couldn't even get a bite anymore. We literally caught every fish in the pond!

Whenever Jase and I were fishing, we always had our own fishing spots. Jase would always try to creep over to my spot if the fish were biting, and we would end up getting in a fight right there on the bank. One day Jase and I were fighting, and

I looked at him and said, "You're a whore." I'd heard the word somewhere and didn't really know what it meant, but I knew it was bad. Jase turned around and looked at me.

"What did you call me?" Jase asked.

"I said you're a whore," I told him.

Jase didn't know what the word meant either, but he still ran as fast as he could back to the house to tell Phil what I had called him. Of course, Phil knew what it meant and I got a whippin' for it.

When we were old enough, I think we got a whippin' nearly every day for fighting and misbehaving. Jase would usually get three licks from Phil, but I would only get one because I would already be screaming and twisting before the first lick ever hit me. Jase always tried not to cry because he thought it made him tougher than me, but I didn't care. It was self-preservation. Hebrews 12:11 says, "No discipline seems pleasant at the time, but painful. Later on, however, it produces a harvest of righteousness and peace for those who have been trained by it." This is so true!

Since I was the baby of the family at the time, my older brothers and their friends could hit harder than me, so I had to come up with a different tactic if I was ever going to get a lick in. I figured the only way to get them good was to throw something at them, then count on my running skills to get away. I had a pretty good throwing arm; must've gotten that from my old man. One day Jase pushed me out of the recliner and stole my seat in the living room.

"I'm the king of the house," Jase yelled proudly.

I was so mad I went to my room and got a twelve-gauge shotgun shell. I was leaning out the door and said, "You're the king of the house, huh?"

"Yep, king of the house," Jase said.

I reared back and hit Jase right in the forehead with the shotgun shell. He caught me at the top of the hill behind our house and shoved dirt in my mouth. I knew if I told Phil and Kay about it, I would be in trouble, too, so I kept my mouth shut and planned my next attack.

Alan was the oldest boy in the family. He was really too big and too much older than us to be fighting with Jase and me, but he always liked to get our fights started and then just sit back and watch. It was like entertainment for him to see how our fights would play out. Al always brought his buddies over to the house to play basketball, and they would start picking on me because I was the youngest. One day I'd had enough of their teasing and grabbed a basketball and hit one of Al's buddies right upside the head with it. I took off running. I knew I couldn't outrun Al, but I was faster than all of his buddies. I ran into the woods and they never caught me.

Al and his friends loved to play tricks on me. Sometimes after I had gone to sleep they would shake me, hollering, "Willie, wake up; it's time for school." I was a pretty heavy sleeper, but I'd wake up, get dressed, brush my teeth, and then go sit on the couch. They would all look at me and just start laughing because it would be like one o'clock in the morning.

WHILE WE ALWAYS SEEMED TO BE IN TROUBLE AT HOME, WE WERE NEVER IN TROUBLE AT SCHOOL OR CHURCH.

Our fights usually ended with a good whipping. We probably deserved even more than we got. We were rough boys who all had a strong, stubborn streak, and while we always seemed to be in trouble at home, we were never in trouble at school or church. We were well-mannered, respectful kids. Kay and Phil say that our teachers always bragged on how good we were. But at home, it seemed like we were always either about to get a whippin' or just coming off one.

Korie: Hearing all these stories about the whippings and fighting always shocks me. It is just so different from the way I grew up. First of all, we didn't call them whippings, we called them spankings, and we did get them, but they were few and far between. I had one brother and one sister and we just were not allowed to fight. I remember pinching my brother when we were little, but that was as bad as it got. I honestly do not remember one time when one of us hit the other because we were mad.

Calling someone stupid or saying "shut up" were absolutely forbidden, as well. One of my mom's favorite sayings was "If you can't say something nice, don't say anything at all." So when my sister and I were mad at our brother, we would give him what we called the "silent treatment." We wouldn't talk to him and basically ignored him for as long as we deemed necessary. It drove him crazy, but we were following Mom's advice. That's pretty much the end of our family's fighting stories!

An example of our getting away without the whipping we deserved, or at least Jase deserved, happened when Kay was over at Granny's house watching *Dallas*. For some reason, Jase thought it would be really funny to lock me out of the house, and I was furious. I kept banging on the door, but Jase had turned the music up loud so he wouldn't hear me. He kicked his feet up on a table and kept yelling, "I can't hear you. I can't hear you." I went to Granny's house and told Kay what Jase had done. Kay went marching back to our house and was hotter than a catfish fry in July. She started banging on the door, but Jase thought it was still me and just kept blaring the music and enjoying having the house to himself. Kay got so angry that she banged on the glass pane and her fist went right through the window, cutting up her hand pretty badly.

This caught Jase's attention. When he saw her hand, he knew he was in big trouble. "When your dad gets home, he's going to whip y'all's butts," Kay told us.

I hadn't even done anything, but Phil didn't usually conduct an investigation to find out who was at fault. He just whipped whoever was in the vicinity of the crime. Jase and I ran back to our room and padded up with anything we could find—socks, underwear, and pillowcases. We sat on our bed with our butts padded, waiting for Phil to get home, certain we were in big trouble. Phil came into the house and saw the bandage on Kay's hand.

"What in the world did you do?" Phil asked her.

"Look at what these boys did," Kay told him. "Jase locked Willie out of the house, and I was banging on the door for him to let us in. My hand went right through the window."

"Kay, that's the dumbest thing I've ever heard. Why would you bang on a glass window?" Phil said.

Phil walked right by her and took a shower. Jase and I were standing there with padded behinds, our mouths wide open with relief.

Phil was always in charge of disciplining us, but sometimes Kay tried to take matters into her own hands. Unfortunately for Kay, she was really an uncoordinated disciplinarian. One day when Phil was out fishing, Kay announced that she was going to whip us. She grabbed a belt that had a buckle on one end and told us to line up for a whipping. Now, Kay never liked whipping us and always closed her eyes when she swung because she didn't want to watch. This time, she reared back and swung and missed, and the buckle flew back and hit her right in the forehead. Jase and I just looked at her, started laughing, and took off running into the backyard. I really don't know how she survived raising us four boys.

Korie: Poor Kay! All that testosterone in one house! Maybe that's why she is so great to us daughters-in-law. She is thankful we took them off her hands. She has definitely enjoyed all of her granddaughters. She has set up a cute little library and a place for tea parties. They have coloring contests and dress-up parties. She didn't get to do any of that with her four boys so our daughters have gotten the full "girly" grandma treatment.

One time, I was painting something outside and came into the house with green paint on my hand. Kay looked at me and said, "I'm going to whip you for bringing paint in the house."

I ran out of the room and put my painted hand on the bed to maneuver my way around her. The bedspread had a green handprint on it for like ten years. I ran through the kitchen and tried to kick open the back screen door, but it wouldn't open, so I ran face-first into it. Before I could get into the backyard, Kay grabbed a fistful of my hair. Kay would always pull your hair; that was the only way she could really control us. We all had little bald spots on our heads from where Kay pulled out our hair. I don't think Jep's hair ever grew back fully. He still has some bald spots back there.

Kay also liked to turn her wedding ring around and knock you upside the head. She would just turn it around and give you a whack if you were out of line. One time, she hit Jase in the forehead with a steel Stanley broom. Jase was messing with me about something, and Kay said she was tired of listening to it. Phil looked at her and said, "Well, do something about it then." So when Jase came around the door, Kay hit him right in the forehead with a broom! Jase was so mad he ran away. No one knew where Jase was after he left; he sat on top of the house like a big rooster for two days.

I was usually the one running away when I was in trouble or mad about something. This generally just involved going to the top of the hill behind our house and staying there until I was cold, hungry, or bored. I would get in trouble for something and then announce angrily, "I'm running away." It would take me thirty minutes to get all my stuff packed to leave,

JASE WAS SO MAD HE RAN AWAY. HE SAT ON TOP OF THE HOUSE LIKE A BIG ROOSTER FOR TWO DAYS.

and Kay would be right there helping me pack. I would ask her, "Mom, where's the Beanee Weenees? Where's my sleeping bag?" She'd run into my room with a can of Beanee Weenees and my sleeping bag, making sure I had everything I needed. Of course, I would always come home as soon as I smelled dinner. I spent more time packing up than I spent away.

For whatever reason, Kay always bought our clothes in pairs. If she bought Jase a blue shirt, I'd get an identical blue shirt. If she bought Jase yellow shorts, I'd get the same pair of yellow shorts. When we were riding the same school bus, Jase would usually get to the school bus stop before me. I always liked to wear the same clothes Jase was wearing because I knew it drove him crazy. Once I saw what Jase was wearing for the day, I would wait until he went outside, then I'd run back in the house and put on the same shirt he had on. Jase would always hit me when I showed up wearing the same clothes as him. Not sure why I did it, because it was a guaranteed lick, but somehow seeing Jase's face was worth it. And although I hate to admit it, maybe there was a little part of me that wanted to be like my older brother.

Phil was good at finding other ways of disciplining us, too.

Every Sunday, our family would load up in Pa's Lincoln Town Car to make the drive to church. There were two bench seats in the car, and eight of us would be packed in there like sardines. It was really too cramped and a fight would undoubtedly break out every Sunday. There was just way too much touching. One time, Phil stopped the car about four miles from our house and told Jase and me to get out. He made us walk those four miles home. We missed Sunday lunch and still got a whipping when we got home. That cut down on the fighting for a while. Somehow after that we figured out how to get along, at least when Dad was in the car.

Kay used to drive an old, beat-up Volkswagen Beetle to work. There was a hole in the back floorboard, which was probably about two feet by three feet wide. She could have been arrested for having kids in the backseat of her car with a hole that big! Every time we went for a drive, Phil would put a board over the hole. Of course, Jase and I would move the board as soon as we pulled out of the driveway, so we could see the road while we were driving. You could have literally stuck your hand down and touched the road. Our favorite thing to do was throw trash out the hole. And that was another thing that usually ended in a whipping when we got home.

Some of my most fun childhood memories are of when my cousins came over. My dad had six siblings, so when the cousins all got together, we were quite the crew. It's safe to say that our cousins didn't grow up the way we did. I'm pretty sure most of them actually lived in subdivisions! I'm sure they thought we were a little backwoods. But they all say they loved it when they got to come visit us. I think they were surprised by how rough we all were, though. We would get in a big circle and two people would wrestle in the middle. It didn't matter if you were a boy or a girl; if you were brave enough to join the fight, you were fair game. I would always end up wrestling my cousin Amy, who was older and bigger than me. But my killer move was putting the leg scissors around her head. If I ever got my legs wrapped around her head, it was lights out. I would wrap my legs around her head and squeeze as hard as I could. One time I was wrestling Amy and she was screaming and crying, and her little brother, Jon, came running up and yelled, "Leave my sister alone!" He was wrapped around my neck and before too long, both of them were just whaling on me. Alan was always the referee, so he had to pull John off my head and send everyone back to their corners.

When we weren't wrestling, we'd take my cousins into our room for a pillow fight. This wasn't just your normal pillow fight. We always had to take it up a notch. There would be one person in the middle of the room with a pillowcase over their head. The other people were holding pillows, whose pillowcases we'd stuffed with blue jeans and anything else we could find. When the lights went out, we would pummel the person sitting in the middle. I don't know how we didn't end up killing each other. I liked to grab my smaller cousins and throw them in a headlock and make them smell

WHEN WE WEREN'T WRESTLING, WE'D TAKE MY COUSINS INTO OUR ROOM FOR A PILLOW FIGHT.

my armpits, too. Those were the good ole days. I was just awful.

Jase and I fought like crazy when we were younger, but as we got older we were really close. We never played organized sports when we were kids because Kay and Phil were so busy trying to get Duck Commander off the ground and make enough money to feed our family that there was no time to chauffeur us kids to baseball or basketball practice. But once we got old enough to drive ourselves, we played every sport we could. We went to a big public high school, so there wasn't much chance of our getting a lot of playing time on the basketball court or in the baseball field. So we played church- and city-league basketball and softball all that we could, and we always played on the same team. Those were some really fun times.

Every year I would play on West Monroe High School's basketball team until church league started. This worked out pretty well. I got out of having to go to PE. I got to practice with the team, so I got really good; then I would quit and play in a league where we could dominate. I was always in charge of assembling our church-league team, which was pretty easy because we only had six players. The team consisted of Jase, Paul, his two brothers, our youth minister, and myself. None of us liked having to sit out of the games, so we didn't carry much of a bench.

We had a really good team. I bet we averaged more than a hundred points per game. In a lot of games, we would run over the scoreboard, so the final score would read forty-two points to twenty-seven, when we'd actually scored one hundred and forty-two points. The scoreboard couldn't even keep up with us! Jase was a set three-point shooter, but he couldn't make layups to save his life. He would run back and always shoot a three-pointer; it was the only shot he ever took or made. In one game, Jase scored thirty-four points—thirty-three came on three-pointers, and he made one foul shot. He always took a high, arching shot and made most of them. I was the point guard of the team, but I liked to shoot the ball, too. When I went to college, I continued to play in recreation leagues, and I played for my fraternity, too—but more about that later.

At any rate, Jase and I had finally figured out a way to turn our competitive natures to sports, and it was serving us well. That is why our last fight—I was sixteen and he was eighteen—came as a surprise to both of us. Our last fight was a bad one. And it was over toast and pizza! I was at home one night and our friend "Curly" Don Foster was sitting on the couch. Curly Don was living with us at the time; one of our friends always seemed to be living with us because Phil and Kay were always willing to help out anyone who needed it. Curly Don and I were watching TV and cooking a frozen pizza in the oven. Jase walked into the house and started making himself some toast, which he then wanted to put in the oven, but my pizza was already in there. We had a small toaster oven, but Jase didn't want to use it because he was making like twelve pieces of toast and he wanted to cook it all at one time.

"I'm going to take your pizza out for a minute and cook my toast really fast," Jase told me.

"Uh-uh, son," I told him. "When my pizza is done, you can have the oven."

"No, I can just change the oven to broil and put my toast right on top," Jase said. "It will cook really quick."

I wasn't having any of it. Both of us grabbed the oven door and started arguing about who was going to cook their meal first. I looked at Jase and shouldered him right into the refrigerator, making a big dent in the door. We were both into watching wrestling, and Jake "the Snake" Roberts was one of our favorite wrestlers. Jase picked me up and put me into Roberts's signature move, the "DDT," picking me up by my pants and lifting me so my legs were straight up in the air. All of a sudden, Jase dropped my head right into a barrel of flour Kay kept in the kitchen. Flour went everywhere. The entire kitchen was covered in a cloud of white!

I put my shoulder into Jase again—I don't know why I kept trying to use that move—and we went flying across the kitchen table. Fortunately, the table didn't break. But the flour barrel splintered and lay flat on the kitchen floor. Jase and I were both covered in flour, and the kitchen was an absolute mess.

Curly Don was sitting on the couch watching us fight.

THE FLOUR BARREL SPLINTERED AND LAY FLAT ON THE KITCHEN FLOOR.

"Don't y'all look like two fine Christians?" he told us, once we settled down enough to hear what he was saying.

I ran out of the house and jumped into Uncle Si's Nissan

truck and drove around for a while. I knew I had to go home and clean up the mess before Phil and Kay got home, or we'd both be in big trouble, but I needed to calm down first. I walked back into the house and apologized to Jase. He did his best to apologize to me (he told me to shut up or something). We've never had a physical fight since. We both realized we were too old and too big to be fighting like that. We could hurt each other or break something else. And to be honest, Curly's comment about our being fine Christians really made an impact on us. Jase and I are brothers, and we realized that wasn't the way God wanted us to be treating each other. Kay was always quoting 1 John 4:20: "For whoever does not love their brother and sister, whom they have seen, cannot love God, whom they have not seen." This was a time in our life when our spiritual walk was growing, and this was a lesson that has stuck with me.

All of our Robertson confidence and stubbornness could serve us well in life, but if we were selfish and didn't use it for the good, it could be to our detriment. We had to figure out how to get along with each other and with others, and we were learning those lessons. Most important, we had to learn how to love as God defines it. As 1 Corinthians 13:4–5 says, "Love is patient, love is kind. It does not envy, it does not boast, it is not proud. It does not dishonor others, it is not self-seeking, it is not easily angered, it keeps no record of wrongs." These were tough lessons for a couple of

WE HAD TO FIGURE OUT HOW TO GET ALONG WITH EACH OTHER AND WITH OTHERS.

country boys, but I'm glad Phil and Kay kept "beating" it into us and Curly Don was there at the right time to remind us.

We shook hands and cleaned up the kitchen. The worst part was that during all the commotion, I burned my frozen pizza.

DUCK SAUSAGE PIZZA

Looking for something weird? Well, here it is! We love pizza at the Robertson household. I have tried all sorts of weird toppings on pizza, and am actually building a pizza oven so I can explore even more. Cooking is all about the exploration. Pizza is the most fun food you can experiment with. Put on whatever you like.

1 tablespoon extra-virgin olive oil
2 garlic cloves, minced
⅛ cup crushed red pepper
1 thin pizza crust, fully baked
1½ cups grated mozzarella cheese
½ cup tomatoes, diced
½ teaspoon dried oregano
⅓ cup green onions, diced
2 smoked duck sausages, sliced
½ cup grated Parmesan cheese

1. Preheat oven to 450 degrees.
2. Mix olive oil, garlic, and red pepper in small bowl.
3. Place pizza crust on baking sheet.
4. Sprinkle pizza crust with mozzarella cheese.
5. Top pizza with tomatoes, oregano, green onions, sliced sausage, and Parmesan cheese.
6. Drizzle olive oil mixture over pizza.
7. Bake pizza about fifteen minutes, or until cheese is melted and crust is brown.

6

ROADKILL

GOD BLESSED THEM AND SAID TO THEM, "BE FRUITFUL AND
INCREASE IN NUMBER; FILL THE EARTH AND SUBDUE IT. RULE
OVER THE FISH IN THE SEA AND THE BIRDS IN THE SKY AND OVER
EVERY LIVING CREATURE THAT MOVES ON THE GROUND."
—GENESIS 1:28

rowing up Robertson meant we were all involved in
the family business, whatever it was at the time. As
we got older that meant helping with duck calls, but
in the early days, Phil had other ways to support his family
while Duck Commander was getting off the ground. Some of
these jobs we enjoyed; others, not so much.

For several years, Dad was in the commercial fishing business, and of course, we all helped out. I started fishing with
Phil when I was about six years old. Jase was older than me, so
he would go out on the boat and be his motorman, while Phil
pulled up the nets.

One of the worst jobs was baiting the nets, which involved
filling socks with rotten cheese. I can still recall the horrible
smell! Phil would buy a fifty-five-gallon drum of rotten cheese,
which was always covered in maggots. We had to reach our

hands down into the drum to scoop the cheese and then shove it into an old sock, gagging the entire time. We filled the socks with the rotten cheese at daybreak, and then Phil would go out and set out the traps. At daylight, Phil and Jase would leave and run the fishing nets until about ten o'clock in the morning. Kay and I would be waiting on the dock for them when they returned, and then Jase and I unloaded the fish and carried them back to the house.

After we put the fish in the back of the truck, Kay and I would then drive to town to go to the markets and sell the fresh fish. One store would take maybe half of the fish, and then we'd head to another store to sell the rest. If we had any fish left after hitting the markets, we'd sit on the side of the road and sell them to the public. I learned pretty quickly that the faster you sold the fish, the faster you got to go home. I learned how to be a good salesman by selling those fish on the side of the road when I was a kid. When it's hot, fish spoil quickly, so there was no time to waste. Once I saw that Mom was more likely to spend some of that cash we made on something I wanted at the store if I did a good job that day, that was just the motivation I needed to work on my craft.

As I got older and wanted to buy more things, I realized selling stuff was my ticket. I mostly wanted an awesome boom box, tapes, and parachute pants. Mom wouldn't buy me the really cool parachute pants with all the zippers; she got me crappy ones that just looked like a windbreaker and didn't have zippers all over them. One summer I sold enough worms on the boat dock to finally get those pants, which looked exactly like Michael Jackson's. They were awesome.

When I was in high school, Phil decided he wanted to get into crawfishing. Like most other things, I'm sure we were doing it unlike anyone else. The problem with crawfish is you can never have enough bait. A crawfish will literally eat anything—as long as it's dead and smells really bad. So if Jase and I spotted a dead possum lying in the road, we'd pick it up and throw it in the back of the truck. We were always looking for roadkill! We took the dead animals home, chopped them up, and threw them into the crawfish nets. Getting the bait became just as fun as the crawfishing.

We had an old deep-freezer in the shop and started throwing roadkill in it. By the end of the summer, the freezer was filled with dead cats, dogs, deer, coons, possums, ducks, and anything else we could find in the road. It smelled awful! We also put tons of snakes in there. We baited snake traps in the water with little perch. We'd pull up the traps at night and then blast the snakes with shotguns. We'd get maybe eight snakes a night; most of them were water snakes but there were always a couple of water moccasins. You never knew what you were going to find in a snake trap.

One night I caught a huge water snake and shot it in the head. I carried it up to the freezer and came back about ten minutes later with my cleaver to chop it up. I reached down in the freezer and grabbed the snake. That snake coiled up and reared its head back with its mouth wide open, ready to strike.

THE DUCK COMMANDER FAMILY

It apparently wasn't dead yet, but it nearly scared me half to death! I threw it down and hit it with the cleaver as hard and as fast as I could. Water snakes aren't poisonous, but that was a big snake. Its bite certainly would have hurt. My heart was racing!

Whenever one of our friends or cousins came to the house, we made them look in the freezer. It looked like a pet cemetery in there! Our family's staple foods were the fish and the crawfish we caught, and you had to have food for the crawfish and bait for the fish as well. The stuff we found on the road worked great for both of these duties, and it was free. We were making lemonade out of lemons, son!

We hunted snakes a lot when I was a kid. In the summer of 1991, the Ouachita River flooded Phil's property pretty badly. Granny and Pa's house was lower to the ground than Phil's, so there was almost six feet of water in their house. Once the snakes got into their house, they couldn't get out. I remember floating around the property on a big Styrofoam block, shooting snakes in the water. We would just sit on the front porch and shoot water moccasins.

Korie: Willie and I were dating by this time, and this was just crazy to me! Because everything was flooded, we had to park up the hill and take a boat to get to their house. They would always have a gun in the boat and would shoot snakes as we rode up. I remember one day when I was down there, Granny needed something from the kitchen in her house, which was literally halfway underwater. Willie got on a block of Styrofoam and paddled into the dark, snake-infested house to retrieve the pot his granny wanted to salvage from her upper kitchen cabinets. It seemed like he stayed in there way longer than he should have. I was scared to death for him, but he came out triumphant and I was proud of my man!

Our crawfish business ended up being pretty lucrative. We sold crawfish commercially to the markets in Monroe. We actually put a boat up on sawhorses and sold live crawfish out of it in the Super 1 grocery store. It was hard keeping the boat filled with crawfish all the time. Like with a snake trap, you never know what you're going to find when you pull up a crawfish trap. You can pick up a trap and find poisonous snakes and about everything else. I picked up a trap one time and there was a big, green river eel in it. This was a good find for crawfish bait. When Phil shoots a duck, he bites its head to make sure it's dead. That eel was still alive, and I didn't have anything with me to kill it, so what's the logical thing to do? I bit the eel's head as hard as I could, and let me tell you something, you can't bite through an eel's head! It's hard and slimy, and just nasty. It took me a week to get the slime out of my teeth! I never tried that again.

When we were growing up with nothing more than an idea in Dad's head for a duck call that sounded exactly like a duck, folks would sometimes look at us with pity and wonder why Dad didn't shave his beard and get a regular job. Some would even poke fun at us. We made it through some really tough times. We were a lot like that roadkill. Most people just saw a dead, stinky animal that had the bad luck to run out in front of the wrong vehicle. But when we saw roadkill, we saw something that could catch a sackful of crawfish. We saw potential in the most unlikely places!

CRAWFISH BALLS

Phil's the king of the crawfish balls. These are his go-to appetizers. When he cooks them, I usually fill up on them before we get to the main dish.

1 stick butter
2 white onions, diced
¼ cup green onions, diced
1 bell pepper, diced
2 stalks celery, diced
8 cloves garlic, diced
¼ cup parsley flakes
1 teaspoon thyme
1 teaspoon basil
2 or 3 dashes of Louisiana hot sauce
salt and pepper to taste
1 pound lump crabmeat (cleaned)
1 pound crawfish tails, cooked
2 eggs
1½ cups Italian bread crumbs
⅔ cup all-purpose flour
peanut oil

1. On medium-high heat in a medium-size pan, sauté butter, white onions, green onions, bell pepper, and celery until vegetables are soft, about eight to ten minutes.
2. Add garlic, parsley, thyme, basil, and hot sauce.
3. Place mixture in a large bowl and season with salt and pepper.
4. Add crabmeat and crawfish tails. Mix well.
5. Beat eggs, add to mixture, and mix well.
6. Add enough bread crumbs to hold mixture together.
7. Make small patties and roll in flour.
8. Deep-fry in peanut oil on medium heat for 3 to 5 minutes or until golden brown.

7

OMELETS

THAT IS WHY A MAN LEAVES HIS FATHER AND MOTHER AND
IS UNITED TO HIS WIFE, AND THEY BECOME ONE FLESH.
GENESIS 2:24

Growing up in the Robertson house, you never had much space or time for yourself. Our house had only two bedrooms, so I shared a room with Alan and Jase for most of my childhood. And then Jep came along, and it was just too crowded. I started looking for other places to sleep, where I wouldn't feel like I was packed in like a sardine.

When I was in middle school, I moved into the cook shack in front of our house, which was screened in at the time. It was during the summer so it wasn't cold, and it had a sink, which was really cool. I had a hot plate out there and cooked my own meals. I even moved into the building where we made the reeds for the duck calls. Neither of these places was very big and they didn't have any insulation, heat, or air-conditioning. They weren't exactly the lap of luxury, but for me, they were mine. And for some reason I always felt like I needed my own space.

Korie: I always thought it was cool that Willie was trying to make his own little place in the world. He liked to fix up his space and paint it. He was a big baseball fan and loved the Los Angeles Dodgers. When he moved into the cook shack, he painted it Dodger blue. Even though it wasn't much, Willie always tried to make it as nice as he could. He put pictures on the walls and would add his own little touches. He tried to have a nice little place to live. I've always been impressed by his ingenuity.

After a while, I figured out I needed to live in a place that was actually attached to the house, so I moved into a small back room that was our laundry room. Korie showed me the laundry room when I visited her house for the first time. I asked her, "Who lives in here? Man, you could fit a double bed in here!"

Korie: I met Willie for the first time when we were in the third grade at Camp Ch-Yo-Ca, the camp I grew up at. Willie and Jase went to my session of the camp, and Alan came for high school week. Kay was cooking in the kitchen that summer, so her boys could attend the camp for free. I remember thinking Willie was the cutest thing I had ever seen and was so funny. We called him by his middle name, Jess, at the time. He had these big dimples and the cutest sideways smile. I had a diary that I never really wrote in, but that summer, I wrote: "I met a boy at summer camp and he was so cute. He asked me on the moonlight hike and I said 'yes'!" I even wrote "Korie Loves Jess" on the bunk of the cabin I was staying in that summer.

Yes, Willie asked me to go on the moonlight hike with him. It was always a big deal every summer figuring out which boy was going to ask you to accompany him on the moonlight hike, and I was thrilled when he asked me! Willie was definitely my first crush. After camp that summer, I didn't see Willie for a couple of years. We went to different schools and his family went to

WILLIE WAS DEFINITELY MY FIRST CRUSH.

a small church out in the country. Our family attended one of the bigger churches in town, White's Ferry Road Church.

When I was in the fifth grade, Ray Melton, the preacher at our church, tried to recruit Phil to start coming to White's Ferry Road. Ray's daughter, Rachel, and I were best friends, and they were going to Phil's house for dinner one night. They invited me to go along. I still remembered Willie from camp, so needless to say, I was just dying to go. I begged my parents to let me go with them. They said yes! I even remember what I wore to Willie's house—a black top with fluorescent green earrings. Don't judge . . . it was the eighties.

When Rachel and I got to the Robertsons' house, the first thing Phil said to us was: "Have you met my boys, Jason Silas and Willie Jess? They'll make good husbands someday. They're good hunters and fishermen." I was so nervous. I could not believe this was happening. The other thing I remember about walking in their home was that Phil and Kay had a sign on their door that said, "Honeymoon in progress." Phil and Kay have never been shy about their honeymooning . . . another thing that shocked me about their family.

Once we had eaten, Willie took us back to his room, which was actually the laundry room. He made us laugh the whole time. He would stick his thumb in his mouth and pretend that he was blowing up his muscles. He did acupressure tricks and showed us our pressure points. This was all very impressive to a couple of fifth-grade girls.

After a while, I decided I was going to try to really impress Korie. I started punching the tiles on the ceiling of the laundry room, which was a trick one of my buddies taught me. I'd rear back and just punch my fist through the ceiling and busted tile would fall over onto the floor. I'm sure she was really impressed.

Korie: After leaving Willie's house, I didn't see him for another two years. In the seventh grade, Phil and Kay finally decided to move the family to our church. Willie called me on the telephone while I was babysitting some of my cousins. We didn't have cell phones at the time, but he had called my house and my mom gave him the number to my aunt's house. He told me they were going to start coming to our church. I was so excited. Willie asked me where I was going to go to college, and I told him I was going to Harding University. Willie thought I said Harvard and told Phil I was going to an Ivy League school. Phil told him: "That's big-time, son."

When the Robertson boys came to our church, everyone was excited because Jase and Willie were definitely the cool new guys. They ended up having a huge influence in our youth group, baptizing nearly a hundred teenagers over the next couple of years. It was incredible. There was tremendous growth in our youth group after they joined our church. Of course, all the girls liked Willie and thought he was cute. I think he dated about every girl in the youth group at one time or another.

OF COURSE, ALL THE GIRLS LIKED WILLIE AND THOUGHT HE WAS CUTE.

One time Willie was dating one of my friends and we were riding on the bus during one of our youth trips, and Willie's girlfriend gave him money to buy her a drink at a gas station. He came back on the bus with a pack of baseball cards and didn't even buy his girlfriend a drink. I remember it made me so mad. I told my friend, "You should break up with him right now." We all thought he was the worst boyfriend ever for doing that!

I'll never forget the first time Willie asked me out. We liked each other off and on through middle school and high school, but we didn't attend the same schools so we never really dated. He was attending West Monroe High School, and I was going to Ouachita Christian School, which is where Phil used to teach. When I was in the eleventh grade (Willie was a year older), he sent one of his friends, Jimmy Jenkins, to ask me out for him. Willie was pretty cocky and all the girls in the youth group were dying to go out with him. But I remembered how he treated my friend, so I told him no. It was a big blow for him, but he needed to be knocked down a few notches. We both continued dating other people over the next year but then were both single around Christmastime during my senior year in 1990.

Willie and I saw each other at the mall a few weeks after Christmas, and it was just one of those moments. Willie was attending seminary school at White's Ferry Road Church and was living with six guys in a small house in town. A couple of days after we saw each other in the mall, Willie walked into his house and there was a chair turned around facing the front door. It had a yellow piece of paper taped to it. It was a message for him, telling him that I had called. I knew that since I had rejected him the last time he asked me out, I would have to be the one to break the ice again. He called me the next day and we went to lunch at Bonanza. It didn't take long before we started dating each other pretty seriously, in January 1991.

Like I said, Willie was living with six other guys in town, but even then, he wasn't exactly living in the house. There was a small storage building out back, which he turned into his own room. He painted all the furniture black and white, and Granny made him a quilt to put on his bed. He had a TV and a window unit for air-conditioning, which he bought with his own money. It was like his little bachelor pad and the first place he could really call his own. Willie was working for my uncle Mac, who owned a cabinet-building shop. Willie worked for Mac throughout high school, cleaning up the shop and doing some woodwork. Mac helped Willie buy his first car, which was a 1980 Ford Mustang. It was bright orange and had white leather seats, which were all torn up, but it got him where he was going.

I used to love going to Willie's little house before school. He would cook me these elaborate omelets and even put a garnish on the top of them. Up till that time, I was never one for waking up early, and I'm still not, for that matter. But during our dating days, I didn't mind getting up early if it meant I got to spend a little more time with Willie. Plus, his cooking really impressed me. Willie's actually very romantic, which a lot of people might not realize. He's written me a ton of love notes and even poems, and he likes to cook for me. Thankfully after twenty years of marriage those things haven't changed.

Willie and I dated for about eight months, and then I was getting ready to leave for school at Harding University. Willie was still attending seminary

> WILLIE'S ACTUALLY VERY ROMANTIC. HE'S WRITTEN ME A TON OF LOVE NOTES AND EVEN POEMS.

school, and I wanted him to go to Harding University with me. But Willie said he wasn't leaving West Monroe. He wanted me to stay in West Monroe with him. We broke up before I left for school in August, and I'm sure he thought I'd find someone else at college, because that's what typically happens when you leave home. Willie called me one night in September 1991 after I had been gone a few weeks and said, "Let's get back together." I knew I loved him, but I told him I wasn't sure about it. He was trying to change my life, and it was really his way or no way. I just didn't know what to do.

"Let me think about it," I said. "I'll call you back tomorrow."

I *was* convinced she'd found someone else. I was telling all my buddies that it was over between us, and I was gathering other girls' phone numbers to prepare myself to move on. I just knew it was over, and I wasn't waiting to hear it from her the next day. I was convinced she wanted to end our relationship but couldn't muster the courage to tell me. Korie called me the next day, and I was ready to tell her that I didn't want to get back together anymore and that our relationship was over. I was certainly going to end it before she ended it. I just knew she already had a new boyfriend at Harding.

"I've got something I want to tell you," Korie told me.

"What do you want to say?" I asked her, deciding I'd better hear her out first.

"Let's get back together," she said.

My ears started buzzing. I threw all the girls' phone numbers in the trash can. About a month later, Korie and I decided we were going to get married.

Korie: I had turned eighteen in October 1991, so legally I was allowed to do whatever I wanted. But I knew I had to call my parents, Johnny and Chrys, to get their permission. We had had some discussions about my getting married that summer that had not gone so well, so I knew they were not going to be excited about it. I mustered up the courage to make the phone call.

"Look, I'm legal, so I'm just going to say it," I told them. "I'm getting married, and you're going to have to be behind me or not."

Of course, my parents told me it was the worst idea ever, and they were naturally worried that I was going to leave school and come home. They asked me to at least wait until I'd finished college. I hung up the phone and called Willie immediately.

"I just told them and it didn't go so well," I blurted out.

"They've already called me and they're on their way over here," he said.

I was trying to save money, so I was living with my brother Alan and Alan's wife Lisa. Korie's parents came to the house to see me, and I sat on the couch with Johnny and Chrys. It was not pretty. The argument was so loud that Alan came out of his room. He looked at us and asked, "What in the world is going on?" Johnny was making all of his arguments, and I was acting like a little punk, twisting his words to put them in my favor, which only made him madder and madder.

Johnny told me that according to studies he'd read, 50 percent of all marriages between young people ended in divorce. He had the articles with him to support his arguments.

"So you're calling that right now?" I asked him. "In all your wisdom, you know we're going to get divorced?"

"I'm not saying that," Johnny told me.

"You just said it," I responded. "You just said half end in divorce. Well, what if we're the good half?"

Then Johnny went on to say that if we got married, he didn't want me coming to him for advice. But then later on in the conversation, he told me I could ask him about anything.

He was completely irrational, and I, of course, had to point that out to him.

"You just said I couldn't ask you for advice," I told him.

He was so mad, I thought he was going to leap off the couch and hit me. Before they left, Johnny looked at me and asked me one last question.

"What's your plan?" he asked.

"What's my plan?" I said to him.

"What exactly is your plan?" he said. "Where are you going to work? Where are you going to live?"

HE WAS SO MAD, I THOUGHT HE WAS GOING TO LEAP OFF THE COUCH AND HIT ME.

"Well, I reckon I'll just buy a trailer and put it on the back property at Phil's house," I told him.

That threw Johnny over the top. He and Chrys stormed out of Alan and Lisa's house, and I was convinced there was no way they were going to give us their blessing to get married. I called Korie to tell her how the meeting went.

"It went terrible," I told her. "We were yelling at each other. It was pretty ugly."

Then Korie had to hang up because her parents were calling her phone. She called me back a few minutes later.

Much to my surprise, her parents told her, "Okay, if you're determined to do this, we're going to support you."

Johnny didn't say much to me for the next few months, during the planning of the wedding, and I knew Korie's parents still didn't like the idea of her getting married so young.

I told Phil that Korie's parents didn't want us getting married and asked him what I should do.

"Here's what I'd do," Phil said, while sitting back in his recliner. "I'd call them up and say, 'Y'all missed that. The wedding was last week when we went to the justice of the peace and got married. Y'all missed the whole thing.'"

Korie: I had never heard my dad yell like he did that night at Willie before that time, nor have I heard it since, but you know daddies and their daughters. I think Willie understands this a little more after having daughters of his own. Thinking back, it makes me laugh to imagine Willie and my dad in that room squaring off. My daddy has since said he didn't have a problem with Willie's marrying me, it just scared him for me to do it at only eighteen. Which was the same age my mom was when they got married, as I kindly pointed out. I had a scholarship to Harding University, which is where both my parents went to school, and that was kind of the plan for my life— to graduate from Harding University and then get married and raise a family. My parents were worried I was going to get married, quit school, and start having babies. But as soon as they decided to support us, that was it. They were completely behind us and wanted to make sure Willie and I would be happy. They

> AS SOON AS MY PARENTS DECIDED TO SUPPORT US, THAT WAS IT. THEY WERE COMPLETELY BEHIND US AND WANTED TO MAKE SURE WILLIE AND I WOULD BE HAPPY.

never said another word about not wanting me to get married so young. Willie and my father rode together to the church before our wedding, and Daddy told him he would never say another word about it, and he hasn't.

We had the biggest, most beautiful wedding on January 11, 1992. It was like a winter wonderland, complete with ice sculptures and white trees. There were probably about eight hundred people at our wedding, and it was a big mix of both of our families. Phil wore corduroy pants and a button-down shirt—he refused to wear a suit or tuxedo—but I didn't care. It was a wonderful wedding. My parents took us to Hawaii the next summer, which was kind of like our honeymoon because we didn't have a chance to take one after we got married.

The day after Willie and I were married, we took another big step in our lives—we moved to Searcy, Arkansas, where Willie started classes with me at Harding University.

CRAWFISH OMELETS

I love crawfish! I have cooked them every way you can. If you don't live someplace where you can catch crawfish in the wild, you can usually get them in the freezer section of the grocery store. If you can't find them there, consider buying them online and having them shipped to you. Crawfish are so delicious, I promise, it will be worth it!

4 large egg whites
2 large eggs
¼ teaspoon Louisiana hot sauce
1 tablespoon water
1 tablespoon fresh chives, chopped
¼ cup cooked crawfish tail meat, chopped
1 tablespoon Phil Robertson's Cajun Style Seasoning
1 teaspoon sour cream
2 tablespoons butter
¼ cup ham, chopped
⅓ cup mushrooms, sliced
2 tablespoons shredded cheddar cheese

1. Combine egg whites, eggs, hot sauce, water, and chives in a small bowl and whisk for 2 minutes.
2. Combine crawfish, Cajun Style Seasoning, and sour cream in a small bowl.
3. In a small skillet melt butter; add ham and mushrooms. Sauté for 3 minutes.
4. Pour egg mixture into skillet. Let it set slightly and cook for 3 minutes.
5. Flip omelet and add crawfish mix onto half of the omelet and cook for 2 minutes.
6. Top with cheddar and cook long enough to melt cheese.

8

CHICKEN STRIPS

BY WISDOM A HOUSE IS BUILT, AND THROUGH UNDERSTANDING
IT IS ESTABLISHED; THROUGH KNOWLEDGE ITS ROOMS
ARE FILLED WITH RARE AND BEAUTIFUL TREASURES.
—PROVERBS 24:3-4

Korie: Willie and I lived in an apartment at Harding University right after we were married. It was just a little one-bedroom apartment, but we loved it. We had the best time decorating it with all of our wedding gifts. After living in the apartment for a semester, we decided that we were wasting money by paying rent every month. We really thought we should buy a house, so we started to look around. Of course, Willie and I were both still taking classes, so we didn't have the money to buy a house by ourselves. Fortunately, my father agreed to help us with the down payment and cosigned the loan for a house. He helped us get our first house, which really meant a lot to us.

We ended up finding a little starter home in Searcy that was still being built, so we were able to pick out the flooring, carpet, and paint color for the walls. The house was only about nine hundred square feet, but we were thrilled to own our first home. We paid about $47,500 for the house and sold it for $60,000 when we moved back to Monroe, so it ended up being a pretty good investment. We had a few other married friends in college, and they would come to our house on the weekends because we were the only ones who owned a house. Willie would cook for everybody, and it was a lot of fun.

I was a year ahead of Willie in college, and I was able to concentrate on school while he worked and took classes. Willie had lots of jobs while we were in college, including working at a bowling alley for a while. If you know Willie, whenever he gets into something, he doesn't ever just do it halfway. He immediately thinks he's going to become a professional at it. So for a while, he wanted to be a professional bowler. Then, after college, he took up golf and was convinced for a while he was going to be a professional golfer.

After I started playing golf pretty regularly, I paid for a lesson from an instructor. The guy had been a professional golfer and even won the Arkansas Open.

"I'm thinking about being a pro golfer," I told him.

He just looked at me and said, "No."

The guy hadn't even seen me swing yet and he was already telling me no.

"You haven't even seen me swing," I told him.

"You ain't got it," he said.

Eventually, I was able to get my handicap down to four, but that was about as close as I ever got to the PGA Tour.

Korie: Willie and I worked together for a little while as telemarketers, and it was the worst job ever. We were in this crowded room with a lot of other people on phones, making cold calls to raise money for leukemia research. At the end of every night, they would show you how much money you had raised. Willie would always raise a ton of money, but I could never get anyone to donate. I was stuck with calling people in New York, while Willie was calling people in Alabama. Nothing against Northerners, but I don't think they are as nice to telemarketers as people in the South. Either that or Willie was just better at it than I was! I think we had that job for about two weeks. It was so horrible.

WILLIE WOULD ALWAYS RAISE A TON OF MONEY, BUT I COULD NEVER GET ANYONE TO DONATE.

Willie also worked as a janitor—he likes to say he was a maintenance supervisor—for a real estate agency, and he went around fixing broken windows, trash disposals, and things like that at the company's rental properties. Willie also worked at an ice cream plant and had to spend most of the day in the freezer. He hated it. He never has liked to be cold.

When I was working at the ice cream plant, Phil came through Arkansas on his way to a speaking engagement. It was the first time Phil had been to Harding University, so he hadn't even seen our new house. I was really pumped that my dad was coming to town because I had a club basketball game that night, and Phil had never seen me play while I was in high school. I went and asked my supervisor at the ice cream plant if I could have the night off since Phil was coming to town. He told me no. I was like, "Screw it. I quit." I hated that job anyway.

It was the only time Phil ever saw me play basketball, and I scored thirty points in the game. It was worth losing the job over. I had a lot of fun playing in the intramural leagues at Harding University. I was the athletic director of my fraternity, so I was allowed to play on every one of our teams if we didn't have enough players. I always played on the A team, but I could play on the lower teams, too. Once I scored seventy-four points on the D team because no one else on the team could really play, so I took just about every shot in the game. I kept begging the coach at Harding University to put me on the school's basketball team. The coach was in his first season, and he was also my badminton teacher. I made a deal with him: If I beat him in a badminton match, he had to put me on the basketball team. I beat him like a drum, but he still didn't put me on the team. I'm still mad at the guy for not holding up his end of the bargain.

Korie: Of course, Willie and I never had any money as married college students. At one point we had to borrow some friends of ours' washer and dryer to do our laundry. To thank them for letting us use their washer and dryer, we took them out to Shoney's one night for dinner. Willie and I cooked in every night; we rarely went out to dinner because we were on such a tight budget. The waiter brought us our bill that night and it was like forty dollars. I didn't even know you could spend forty dollars at Shoney's! Daddy had worked with Willie and me on keeping a budget. He taught us to write down all of our expenses so we could see how we were spending our money. If we ever had to borrow any money from Dad, he always wanted to see a plan for how we were going to pay him back. Daddy really taught us some valuable lessons about money. We budgeted about sixty dollars a week for food. After paying the bill at Shoney's, we had about twenty dollars left for the entire week!

Whenever Willie and I went to the grocery store to buy food for the week, there was always a big argument at the checkout lane. If we had any money left in our budget, Willie would want to buy baseball cards or a *Star Trek* book. He has always been a big collector. I wanted to buy a magazine like *People* or *Entertainment Weekly,* and we never had enough money to buy both. We'd fight over who was going to get to spend our disposable income, which ended up being about three or four dollars a week. These are some of the things you fight over when you get married at eighteen and nineteen!

When we were newlyweds, our favorite meal was chicken strips and macaroni and cheese. We would buy a big bag of frozen Tyson chicken strips and fry them in a Fry Daddy. When they came out we would season them, then dip them in butter. Willie would make these special sauces for the

chicken strips and we'd always have a box of Kraft macaroni and cheese with them. We rotated the chicken strips
with chili dogs and, of course, fried bologna sandwiches, and that would be our
meals for the week. Sometimes we would
even splurge on thick-cut bologna. Willie
tried to get me to eat fish sticks, but I'd
never eaten them in my life. I just couldn't
stomach eating frozen fish out of a box.

WHEN WE WERE
NEWLYWEDS,
OUR FAVORITE
MEAL WAS
CHICKEN STRIPS
AND MACARONI
AND CHEESE.

When we were taking classes, we'd come home between
classes and eat lunch together every day. We would cook
lunch and then watch *Matlock* together and see who could
guess the killer. Willie bought a little white truck from one of
our professors for seven hundred dollars. The best part about
the truck was it still had a faculty parking sticker on the wind-
shield. We were so excited we could park the truck in the faculty lots when we went to class. Because we were married,
we could even write excuses for each other when we were
sick. Willie always seemed to catch a cold during March Mad-
ness and on the opening day of baseball season.

During our last year at Harding University, we spent the
summer in a study-abroad program in Florence, Italy. It was
an unbelievable experience and was our first time really being
away together. We traveled all over Europe on a Eurail pass.
We didn't have any money for hotel rooms, so we would just
sleep on trains and wake up the next morning in a new country. It was so exciting. As part of our studies, we had to visit
certain museums and write essays on the art we saw. I was

an art education major, so I loved every bit of this part of our trip, but it was a totally new experience for Willie. By the end of the trip, he said he had more culture than the yogurt section of the grocery store!

Willie and I are both pretty directionally challenged, so we spent most of our time lost. We would jump in a bus that seemed to be going in the right direction and end up having to walk for miles to get back to town. We were both super skinny from all the walking when we got back, despite the good Italian food we ate while we were there.

We had the best time, but there were a few scary moments, as well. One night we were sleeping on the train heading to Barcelona, Spain. We were traveling through the south of France and a group of thieves were on the train. Willie was sleeping with his feet on the door, so every time they would try to open the door he would wake up and they would run off. One time, he didn't feel the door open and the thieves grabbed the backpack of one of the girls who was traveling with us. Willie jumped up and started chasing them through the train! They dropped the backpack, but Willie kept chasing them through a couple of cars. I was standing there thinking, "What's going to happen if he catches them!" Luckily, Willie had that same thought, gave up the chase, and came back to our car. He didn't sleep the rest of the night; he just sat up and protected us. What a man!

Another exciting but scary adventure happened in Salzburg, Austria, where we were staying at a youth hostel named Stadtalm Naturfreundehaus. It was at the top of a mountain that surrounded the city and had the most beautiful view. It had bunk beds in the rooms and only had one bathroom that everyone shared. You had to put coins in the shower for the water to come out. It only gave you like two minutes of water. I remember calling down the hall to Willie to bring more coins. Two minutes wasn't quite long enough.

The way you got to the hostel was on an elevator through the middle of the mountain. One night, we got back to the elevator about eleven thirty P.M., after exploring the city, only to find that the elevator closed at eleven P.M. We had no idea what to do. We certainly didn't have enough money to get another hotel room for the night, so we went back into the town and asked around to see if there was any other way to get up there. We found out there was a staircase that would get you there eventually, but it was a long walk up the mountain. We didn't have any other choice. We walked what seemed like forever. At one point, we passed a guy in a trench coat, just sitting by himself on a bench on the trail. We were totally freaked out. Well, I was, at least. We finally got to the top about two A.M. We ended up sitting outside under the stars and talking once we got there, and we thanked God for keeping us safe. It ended up being really fun and romantic, but I was scared to death walking in a foreign city up a creepy trail in the middle of the night.

When I finished school at Harding University in 1995, we moved back to West Monroe. Willie still had a year left of school, so he enrolled at Northeast Louisiana University (which is now the University of Louisiana at Monroe) and he took a job working at Camp Ch-Yo-Ca. Willie probably could have gone to work part-time for Duck Commander, but he'd helped Phil make duck calls when he was a child, so at this point he really wasn't interested in doing it again. Duck Commander was still pretty small, and Jase and their friend Bill "Red Dawg" Phillips were already working there. Duck Commander couldn't afford to take on another full-time employee, but Willie still helped out at Duck Commander from time to time, especially during hunting season, and we would always go to SHOT Show—the big hunting-industry trade show—with the whole family every January. Willie would drive a seventeen-passenger van to SHOT Show and would work as their driver.

Willie really did some unbelievable things with Camp Ch-Yo-Ca, which was a nonprofit and seemed to lose a lot of money every year. Willie was determined to make sure the camp at least broke even financially every year. He studied kinesiology at Harding University and then went into the health and human performance program at Northeast Louisiana. The program required him to take some business courses. Willie took the camp's deficit from about $150,000 to $5,000 in a couple of years. The kids would come to camp for about six weeks during the summer, but Willie started renting the camp's facilities to churches and youth groups during the off-season. He started a program for schools to bring their classes to the camp for nature hikes, and he even added tennis courts, hiking trails,

> WILLIE WAS DETERMINED TO MAKE SURE THE CAMP AT LEAST BROKE EVEN FINANCIALLY EVERY YEAR.

and other amenities. He was very creative in finding ways to create new revenue for the camp. Willie learned how to operate a business on a budget and the camp proved to be a good training ground for him.

Another man helped out at the camp who made a big impact on Willie during this time. His name was Dewie Kirby. He was the dad of my uncle on my mom's side. He was retired and moved across the street from us at the camp to help do maintenance and help Willie take care of the camp. Willie and Dewie worked together on many projects, and Willie grew to love Dewie as another father figure who taught him about work and family.

I was pregnant with our first child when we moved back to Monroe. Our oldest son, John Luke, was born in October 1995, and then Sadie came along not long after in June 1997. To help make ends meet, Willie started working as a youth minister at our church in addition to keeping his job at Camp Ch-Yo-Ca. He was great with teenagers and college-aged students and always had a few teens working with him at camp. He remembered how important it was that Mac gave him a job as a teenager and took the time to teach him how to work. He tried to do the same for others.

During this time, the pull to get more involved in the family business of Duck Commander was coming over us. Since the camp business was seasonal and everything pretty much shut down in the wintertime—which was the busy time for Duck Commander—we were able to help out some and do several things from our home. We were fortunate to be able to do this as a family and spent quite a bit of time together with our babies.

I tried to find ways to help us financially during this time. After John Luke was born, I was a stay-at-home mom but still found ways to utilize my art degree. I started making hand-painted duck calls. I numbered them and had Phil autograph cards saying they were limited editions of five hundred each. I painted sitting mallard, flying drake, and wood duck editions. They ended up selling in stores like Bass Pro Shops and Cabela's. While the babies were sleeping, I would paint the duck calls, put them in a package with moss and a card, and ship them out the door.

I really think the first few years of our marriage were Willie's formative years. He still wasn't sure what he wanted to do with his life, whether he wanted to preach, work for the family business, or do something entirely on his own. I knew that whatever he decided he would do it with all his heart and be successful at it. This was a time for him to test out and find what he really wanted to do. We were eating frozen chicken strips, but we were eating them together and finding ways to make them delicious.

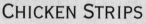

CHICKEN STRIPS

I can't hunt chicken. Well, I guess I could, but I don't think it would be much fun, but I do like to eat it from time to time. This is one of those popular dishes that kids love. Can't go wrong here.

2 pounds chicken tenderloins
1 egg
½ cup buttermilk
1 cup all-purpose flour
1½ teaspoons garlic powder
½ teaspoon paprika
1 tablespoon Phil Robertson's Cajun Style Seasoning
1 teaspoon salt
1 teaspoon pepper
Peanut oil (about 3 inches in pan)
1 cup butter, melted

1. Whisk egg and buttermilk in a small bowl.
2. Combine flour, garlic powder, paprika, Cajun Style Seasoning, salt, and pepper in separate bowl.
3. Dip chicken tenderloins in egg mixture and then flour mixture.
4. Heat oil in skillet to 375 degrees.
5. Cook tenderloins for three minutes on each side or until no longer pink.
6. Drain chicken strips on paper towels.

9

DUCK GUMBO

"FOR I KNOW THE PLANS I HAVE FOR YOU," DECLARES
THE LORD, "PLANS TO PROSPER YOU AND NOT TO HARM
YOU, PLANS TO GIVE YOU HOPE AND A FUTURE."
—JEREMIAH 29:11

Phil's duck gumbo takes a long time to make. It starts
at four A.M. on a wet, cold Louisiana morning during
duck season. Well, it actually starts a long time before
that day, sometime in the heat of summer, when he's out on
the land pumping water into the hole in front of the blind
or repairing a torn-down blind. But let's take all of that for
granted for a moment and start with the day he actually kills
the ducks for the gumbo.

Phil wakes up in the early-morning hours of a cold December day and pulls on his hunting gear. He walks out of his bed-
room to find Jase, Uncle Si, Godwin, Martin, and me walking
through the door to drink black coffee and discuss our plan
for the day. Phil guzzles his coffee and then loads up the truck
with decoys, shotgun shells, and his favorite gun. He puts his
duck calls around his neck and his black Lab, Trace, happily

jumps into the truck. Phil then drives to the land, loads up on the boat, and climbs into a blind to sit and to wait. He waits until the sun comes up for the legal shooting time to begin, and then waits some more for ducks to fly by. And when they do, Phil blows his calls, with Jase calling along beside him, helping to replicate the exact sound of the ducks for the decoys in the spread. Phil watches and listens for the familiar sound of the ducks turning, locking their wings, and changing their patterns to check out what is below. His heart starts pumping when he realizes the ducks have heard them and are coming his way, then he waits some more. He waits until the ducks are right in front of the blind and then calls out, "Cut 'em!" Phil and the rest of the hunters in the blind raise their shotguns and shoot. Trace takes off through the water, excited for the opportunity to do his job, bringing the bounty back to the blind. Now Phil has his ducks for the gumbo.

Next, Phil brings the ducks back to the house and picks their feathers clean. Then he carefully cuts them into pieces for the gumbo, cautious not to lose any of the precious meat. Now Phil can finally begin to make the roux. Building a successful family business is a lot like making a great gumbo.

Phil started duck hunting when he was a kid. He used a P. S. Olt duck call, which was very popular among duck hunters at the time. In the late 1880s, Philip Olt converted a chicken coop on his family's farm into a wood shop and started making duck calls. Olt's D-2 Duck Call and A-50 Goose Call were some of the first manufactured duck calls in the world, which is why he is often called the "father" of the manufactured call.

Phil had a gift for making his calls sound better, and his hunting buddies always insisted that he tune their calls, too. When Phil was hunting with his friend Al Bolen in 1972, Big Al watched him make a long-hailing call as he was trying to turn a flock of mallard ducks within shooting range.

"Man, you weren't calling those ducks," Big Al told him. "You were *commanding* them!"

And so . . . Duck Commander was born.

On the day Phil officially announced he was starting Duck Commander, he told Kay, Granny, and Pa that he was going to sell one million dollars' worth of duck calls. Of course, they all thought he was crazy and went back to eating dinner. It took many years for Duck Commander to get off the ground. Phil always likes to say he's a low-tech man living in a high-tech world, and he didn't know very much about woodworking, marketing, or manufacturing when he started. But Phil had a dream, and his veins were filled with determination and patience, which is probably more valuable than anything else.

"MAN, YOU WEREN'T CALLING THOSE DUCKS. YOU WERE *COMMANDING* THEM!"

When Phil was getting started with his company, he enlisted the help of Tommy Powell, who went to church with us at White's Ferry Road Church. Tommy's father, John Spurgeon Powell, made duck calls in a small wood shop, and Phil took him his drawings for the world's first double-reed duck call. John Powell looked at Phil's specifications and told him it wouldn't work.

"It's too small," Powell told him.

But Powell told Phil if he could get a block of wood properly bored, he was willing to give his duck call a try on his lathe. Phil took a block of wood that was about three inches thick and six inches long to West Monroe High School's woodworking shop, where he worked out a swap with the shop teacher. In exchange for four dressed mallard ducks, the shop teacher drilled a hole in Phil's block of wood. Phil took the wood block to Powell, who turned on his lathe and produced the first Duck Commander duck call.

With a working prototype, Phil set out to make his dream come true. He borrowed $25,000 from the bank with the help of Baxter Brasher, an executive at Howard Brothers Discount Stores, and purchased a lathe for $24,985. Later, Phil learned the lathe was only worth about $5,000 and had been built in the 1920s! The lathe was transported from Memphis to Monroe, and Phil picked up the heavy machinery at the train station with a borrowed dump truck. Phil drove the lathe to our house and cut out the wall of an outbuilding with a chain saw. Somehow, he was able to drag the lathe into his shop by tying a come-along to a tree. Once everything was in place, Phil put a sign outside the shop that read DUCK COMMANDER WORLDWIDE.

PHIL PUT A SIGN OUTSIDE THE SHOP THAT READ DUCK COMMANDER WORLDWIDE.

Phil didn't even have an instruction manual for the lathe or templates to cut the wood for his calls. Obviously, there was a lot of on-the-job learning. But it didn't take Phil long to get a production line going, and Alan, Jase, Kay, Pa, and I were his crew. When I was young, we spent most of our days helping him manufacture and package the duck calls. In the beginning, Phil cut end pieces out of cedar and barrels out of walnut. He tried all kinds of wood; he even brought back cypress logs from his fishing runs and cut them into blocks.

Our assembly line was out on the porch of our house, which was screened in at the time. Pa was always there helping Phil. One of the earliest problems with Phil's duck call was that the two reeds had a tendency to stick together. Pa told Phil that he should put a dimple in the reeds to keep them separated. Phil took a nail and put a dimple in the reeds with a hammer. Uncle Si still uses the same technique in our reeds today.

The great thing about Duck Commander is that it was a family business from the start and remains that way today. When I was younger, I helped by sweeping up the sawdust in the shop. My oldest brother, Alan, used a band saw to cut the ends of the calls, and Phil ran a drill press to set up and calibrate the end pieces. Jase and I also dipped the calls in polyurethane and then dried them on nails. Once the calls were dry, we sanded them down to a fine finish. I was embarrassed going to school because my fingers were always stained brown from tung oil. There were always rows of hard tung oil drippings in our yard.

The especially bad part for Jase and me was when Phil figured out that the more you sanded and dipped the calls, the shinier they were. That meant more dipping for us! Phil would tell us, "Hey, go dip the duck calls. There's about twenty of them." But when he said there were twenty or twenty-five, it always meant there were seventy-five to one hundred, and "thirty or thirty-five" meant there were probably one hundred and fifty. Phil was a notorious foreman on the duck-call assembly line.

Last, and most important, Phil blew every single call to make sure it sounded like a duck. From day one, Phil was convinced his duck call sounded more like a live duck than anything else on the market, and he wanted to make sure his products were always perfect. Duck Commander still follows that same principle today.

PHIL BLEW EVERY SINGLE CALL TO MAKE SURE IT SOUNDED LIKE A DUCK.

In the early days, the work never seemed to stop. My brothers and I cut boxes and folded them to package the duck calls. I don't think child labor laws applied to us down on the mouth of Cypress Creek. When it was dark and you went inside to eat dinner and watch TV, you started folding boxes. We sat in the living room folding boxes, and they'd be scattered across the room. There was a plastic sleeve with a logo that we slipped over the boxes. The Duck Commander logo—which is now famous—is a mallard drake with wings cupped and legs lowered, looking down at the land. The logo was printed in gold on a green background and was placed on each of the calls. Phil's name was also on the package, along with our home address.

Duck Commander is a lot like Phil's duck gumbo. The

gumbo is perfect only when it has the right blend of ingredients—garlic, bell peppers, onions, shallots, sausage, spices, and, of course, duck. When my brothers and I were growing up, everyone in our family played an important role in the evolution of Duck Commander, and we still do today. If you take the onions or sausage out of Phil's gumbo, it's not going to taste nearly as good. And if you were to take Alan, Jase, Jep, or Uncle Si out of Duck Commander, the company wouldn't be as good as it is today.

Korie: The entire business was run out of the Robertsons' house. When Willie and I were dating, every time I went to their house, I was folding boxes. Phil is very charismatic and people love to be around him, and he learned pretty early that if you were willing to feed people, they were usually willing to work. Kay and Phil often had big fish fries at their house, and they would usually turn into packaging parties. People would call their house from stores to place orders. People from Wisconsin would call to buy one or two duck calls. When Willie was a little kid, he was answering the phone, taking orders. Customers called at all hours of the day. Willie answered the phone and always said: "Duck Commander, can I help you?" It was usually somebody in Texas or California wanting a duck call. Willie grabbed a napkin or paper plate and wrote down the order. There was always a big stack of paper plates or napkins sitting on the counter with orders written on them. The next day, Kay got the orders together and shipped them out at the post office.

I get asked this question a lot: why do Willie and Jase call their parents by their first names? I've asked Willie and he doesn't even know the answer, but we think it is because growing up when the business was being run out of their home, they would have to take these business calls for stores and orders on their home phone. The boys began referring to them as Phil and Kay in the business conversations and it just stuck. Jep, the youngest, didn't work as much in the family business as a kid, because he was born so much later and by that time they had more employees to take the phone calls, and he still calls them Mom and Dad. So that's our theory as to why Jase and Willie call them Phil and Kay. I can assure you it is not a sign of disrespect.

With a finished product, Phil hit the road in a blue and white Ford Fairlane 500 that once belonged to Kay's grandmother—Nanny. Phil liked to call the trips his "loop," and he was usually gone for about a week. With his calls stacked in the backseat and the trunk, Phil made a big circle around southern Arkansas, East Texas, West Mississippi, and into all parts of Louisiana, selling his duck calls at any sporting goods store or hunting shop he could find. He sold his first duck calls to Gene Lutz of Gene's Sporting Goods Store in Monroe.

In Lake Charles, Louisiana, Phil met Alan Earhart, who had been making the Cajun Game Call for years. Earhart liked Phil and agreed to make two thousand Duck Commander calls for him at the price of two dollars each. Phil would still cut the reeds and put the calls together, blowing each one before it went out the door, but Earhart cut the barrels. Phil figured if Earhart could handle a part of the manufacturing for a while, he would have more time to concentrate on sales calls and spreading the Duck Commander name.

Phil sold about $8,000 worth of Duck Commander calls in the first year. By the second year, his sales increased to $13,000; they rose to $22,000 in the third. By the fourth year, Duck Commander grossed about $35,000.

About five years into running Duck Commander, Phil realized many of his longtime customers were going out of business. There was a new superstore chain called Wal-Mart (as it was spelled then) moving into a lot of towns in Arkansas and Louisiana. As soon as a Wal-Mart store went up, a sporting goods or hardware store closed its doors a few months later. Phil realized that if Duck Commander was going to survive, he had to figure out a way to get his duck calls into this new chain. After initially being told that he had to go through Wal-Mart's corporate office, Phil persuaded a local store manager to buy six of his duck calls. He took the Wal-Mart sales order to the next Wal-Mart down the road and showed the manager what the other store had bought, and there he sold a dozen more. Eventually, Phil was selling $25,000 worth of duck calls to Wal-Mart alone, selling to them one store at a time, and his business was starting to expand.

One day, Phil got a call from one of Wal-Mart's executives.

"How did you get your product in our stores?" the man asked.

"Store to store," Phil told him.

"Well, you have to go through me," the man said. "I'm the buyer."

Somehow, Phil won over the buyer and the man sent him an authorization letter, which allowed him to sell his duck calls to any Wal-Mart store that wanted them. The next year, Phil even persuaded the buyer to purchase bulk orders of Duck Commander calls to distribute to stores across the country. Eventually, Duck Commander was selling $500,000 worth of duck calls to Wal-Mart each year. Phil's dream was beginning to come true.

Phil was a pioneer because he wasn't afraid to take risks. I don't think anyone ever quite understood what he was doing. But Phil was very self-confident and believed in his dream. He was a real showman and when he took his calls on the road, he was a great salesman. When he started the business, Phil actually carried an audio recording of live mallard ducks. He played the tape and then blew his call, which convinced customers that his calls truly sounded exactly like a duck, thus were the best on the market.

PHIL WAS A PIONEER BECAUSE HE WASN'T AFRAID TO TAKE RISKS.

Phil was always a dreamer and a visionary and was focused on the big picture. He knew he could make his dream come true by pulling his family together.

When I think of the journey it took for Duck Commander to get to where it is today, I think of it as a lot like Phil's duck gumbo. You can't go to the grocery store and buy all the ingredients. Well, I guess you could, but it wouldn't taste the same. There are no shortcuts for the kind of duck gumbo my family makes. It takes hard work, patience, and perseverance on the days when you sit in the blind and wait and the skies are clear. And you need strength of character on the days when it's cold and rainy and you wish you had stayed in bed. It takes camaraderie and a willingness to work with the other hunters in your blind to set up the decoys and call in unison. And, most important, it takes a passion and a love for what you are doing to see it to the end. All of these traits were present in making Duck Commander what it is today and are still present in the way we work.

> THERE ARE NO SHORTCUTS FOR THE KIND OF DUCK GUMBO MY FAMILY MAKES.

There have been tough times in the life of Duck Commander. Times when we've lost big accounts, years when the duck numbers were down because of the weather in Canada, and even times when we didn't know where we would get the money to make it through another season. There have been times when we had to bring in extra help to get an order out on time and times when we had to let someone go because there was not enough work or money to pay them. There have been times when the money came at just the right moment to pay the light bill.

Phil tells about one such time in the early days of Duck Commander. The bank note was due and Kay informed him that they simply did not have the money to pay it. They were broke. Phil says that he tried everything he could think of to get the money to pay the debt. He and Kay were at the end of their rope. Kay was in tears with worry over what was going to happen to all they had worked for. Phil remembers telling Kay, "Let's go check the mailbox, maybe there will be a check in there." Kay told him, "There is no reason to look because no one owes us anything."

Phil knew it wasn't likely, but for some reason, he felt like they needed to look. They walked to the mailbox together and pulled out an envelope postmarked from Japan. It was an order for duck calls with a check for eight hundred dollars to prepay for them. It was exactly the amount they needed to pay the bank note! Duck Commander had never sold a duck call to Japan before then and as far as I know has never sold one since. But somehow, at a time when Phil and Kay needed it, the Lord provided. That's the only way to explain it.

Phil remembers another time that same eight-hundred-dollar bank note was due and once again there was no money to pay it. This time Phil went out to run the nets, hoping to catch enough fish to sell to at least take care of part of the payment. He took his boat out and began setting lines. The fish started biting before he even put any bait on the hooks! He says he pulled fish in hand over fist. He filled up his boat in no time and had more than enough to pay the bill with the sale of the fish he caught that day. Again, Phil says he never saw anything like what happened that day before or since.

The truth is, the Lord has always provided. Like He cares

Days before Willie came into this world. Alan, Jase, Kay, and Phil, 1972.

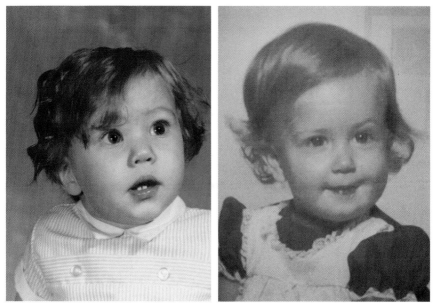

Willie's baby picture, 1972. Check out that hair!

Korie's baby picture, 1973.

Willie with his granny, 1975.

Korie with her brother and Papaw Howard, who taught her how to fish and skin a squirrel (and push a wheelbarrow). Alton, Korie, and Ryan Howard.

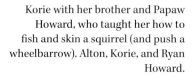

Robertson family photo taken for the church directory, 1988. Clockwise from top: Phil, Alan, Jase, Kay, and Willie. *(Photograph © Olan Mills Photography)*

Uncle Si hanging out on the steps with Willie and Jase, 1974.

Korie's family's annual ski trip, Colorado, 1990. Left to right: John, Chrys, Ashley, Korie, and Ryan Howard.

The Robertson men BTB (before the beards) playing golf on the family beach vacation in 2001. Willie, Jase, Alan, and Jep.

Willie and Korie. Young love! Camp Ch-Yo-Ca, 1991.

Willie and Korie on their wedding day, January 11, 1992. So happy! *(Photograph © Lamar Photography)*

Korie and Willie on their honeymoon trip to Hawaii, 1992.

Korie's 1995 college graduation from Harding University, with proud grandparents Luther and Jo Shackelford.

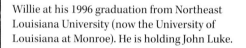

Willie at his 1996 graduation from Northeast Louisiana University (now the University of Louisiana at Monroe). He is holding John Luke.

December 15, 2001, the first time Willie and Korie held Little Will. They were in awe of this sweet little boy!

Willie with Sadie and John Luke on the steps of the house at Camp Ch-Yo-Ca, 1998.

Willie before the beard, rocking blond tips. Left to right, Sadie, Korie, Willie, and John Luke at Gulf Shores, Alabama, in 2000.

John Luke and Sadie in 2002 at their school's Grandparents' Day, getting hugs from their two grandmas, Kay Robertson and Chrys Howard.

Korie with the kids, 2003: (clockwise) John Luke, Sadie, Bella, and Will.

The first year Rebecca was with Korie and Willie for their annual beach vacation at Gulf Shores, Alabama, 2006. First row: Rebecca, Korie, Bella, Will, and Willie. Back row: Sadie and John Luke.

Family beach trip to Gulf Shores, Alabama, 2012. Front row: Rebecca, Bella, Korie, and Sadie. Back row: Will, Willie, and John Luke.

Sadie and Will in 2012. So proud of how the kids love each other.

Sadie and John Luke celebrating the Fourth of July, 2012.

Papaw Phil in 2012 teaching Bella about building duck blinds.

Papaw Phil with the grandkids, 2005. Back row: John Luke and Reed (Jase's son). Front row: Bella, Will, Phil, Sadie, and Cole (Jase's son).

Family trip to California, 2012. Left to right: Rebecca, John Luke, Bella, Sadie, and Will.

All the grandkids and great-grandkids with their awesome Mamaw Kay. Back row: Cole, John Luke, Reed, Kay, Sadie, Bailey, and Will. Front row: Bella, Lily, Merritt, River, Carly, Priscilla, and Mia.

Willie and Phil in 2006, posing for the label for our seasoning bottles.

Phil and Willie in the "Boss Hog mobile" for a Benelli commercial, 2010.

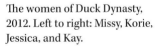

The women of Duck Dynasty, 2012. Left to right: Missy, Korie, Jessica, and Kay.

Si with his now-famous glass of tea at Willie and Korie's house, July 4, 2012.

Korie's first deer! Willie was proud. Olla, Louisiana, 2010.

The Duckmen had a good day in the blind on Robertson land, 2011. Jase, Phil, and Willie.

Willie doing a photo shoot for Buck Commander Weaver Scopes.
(Photograph © Lee Kjos Photography 2011)

John Luke and Willie
in 2011, getting ready to
pick the ducks.

Willie singing "Take Me
Out to the Ball Game" at an
Atlanta Braves game in 2010.
He is on top of the dugout
during the seventh-inning
stretch.

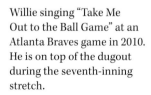

Willie and Korie in 2012
accepting the Golden Moose
Award for Duck Commander.

Willie and Phil's first late-night appearance. *(Photograph © Conan O'Brien, 2012)*

Phil, Korie, and Willie in 2012 on Sunset Boulevard with the Duck Dynasty billboard.

The Duck Dynasty photo shoot. It was freezing that day! Kay, Phil, Willie, Korie, Si, and Jase.

Phil and Si taking Sadie out to run the nets and teach her a few life lessons. *(Photograph © A&E, 2011)*

First time on the red carpet for A&E's Upfront, 2012. Willie, Korie, Phil, Kay, and Si.

Korie in 2012 with two women who are great examples of godly wives and mothers—Korie's mother and grandmother, Chrys Howard and Jo Shackelford.

Phil and Kay with all their boys at the 2012 Duck Commander 40th Anniversary Party. Jep, Alan, Phil, Kay, Jase, and Willie.

for the birds in the air and clothes the lilies in the field, He has cared for us. We haven't done everything right. We didn't have all the right business plans, goals, or budgets. Sometimes, we didn't know how a bill was getting paid until the very last minute, but we always had faith that He would provide. Miracles like the two

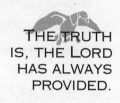

THE TRUTH IS, THE LORD HAS ALWAYS PROVIDED.

described above didn't happen every time. Sometimes, we had to hold our checks, and there were times when Kay had to borrow at high interest rates or make deals with one store to get money at a time she needed it. But there was always that faith that the Lord would provide.

I think that's the only way you can ever be truly successful in this world. You have to acknowledge that it is from above. And you have to have the confidence that even if you lose it all, things will be okay. You have to be willing to fail, and all the while work your tail off to succeed. You have to continue doing the work, believing in what you are doing, and most important, keeping your faith in who you are. The faith of our family is not in the things we have. Our confidence is not in the monetary success we have gained. It is in the One who made us and who is there for us in good times and bad.

Phil's duck gumbo is never finished until he knows it's absolutely perfect. In many ways, Duck Commander is a lot like his gumbo. It took forty years to build Duck Commander into what it is today. Phil has always had a lot of perseverance and patience, which are valuable attributes to have in everything from business to cooking to hunting. Let's face it: most people today wouldn't take a few days to make duck gumbo. They go out and buy a mix and throw it together. But if you wait and you're truly patient, the end result is going to be something that is unbelievably spectacular and special.

DUCK GUMBO

This is Phil's duck gumbo recipe. Making gumbo is an art and Phil's is a masterpiece. It takes time and patience to make it just right.

8 ducks
salt and pepper to taste
1 bay leaf
3 cups flour
3 cups peanut oil
3 white onions
3 green onions
handful of fresh parsley
1 clove garlic, chopped
cayenne pepper to taste
Phil Robertson's Cajun Style Seasoning to taste
sausage

1. Place fully cleaned ducks into a large pot filled with water.
2. Add salt, black pepper, and bay leaf to pot.
3. Boil ducks for 2½ hours.
4. While ducks are boiling, prepare roux in another large pot: For 8 ducks, mix 3 cups of flour and 3 cups of peanut oil.
5. After stirring flour and oil to a consistent paste, heat on medium low.
6. Stir thoroughly until color is a dark chocolate brown. (Should take 35 to 40 minutes.)
7. Dice up white onions, green onions, and parsley.
8. Once roux is dark brown, mix in onions and parsley. (Watch out for the steam!)
9. Add garlic.
10. After ducks have boiled for 2½ hours, take them out of pot (saving broth) and separate meat from bone.
11. Take broth and fill roux pot just over half full.
12. Turn heat up to boiling again.
13. When the peanut oil rises to top of pot, remove it with spoon.

14. Sprinkle a small amount of cayenne pepper and Cajun Style Seasoning into pot.
15. Dice up sausage into nickel-size pieces.
16. Dump duck meat and sausage into gumbo.
17. Let it simmer for 3 to 4 hours.
18. Serve gumbo over rice and enjoy!

10

FROG LEGS

LET PERSEVERANCE FINISH ITS WORK SO THAT YOU MAY
BE MATURE AND COMPLETE, NOT LACKING ANYTHING.
—JAMES 1:4

Many things in life—whether it's food, business, or even someone's personality—slowly evolve over time. They don't necessarily get better overnight, but if you keep working at them and stay focused, chances are they're going to end up being better than when you started. Take for instance my recipe for frog legs. When I was growing up, Kay's frog legs were one of my favorite meals. But as I got older, I started experimenting with ways to cook frog legs and added my own personal touch to her recipe. Kay has probably never heard of garlic-infused grape-seed oil (she's never used anything but butter or Crisco), but that's what I like to use to fry my frog legs. And for the record there are many infused olive oils I like using nowadays. Kay still doesn't understand how they "infuse" oil, but I tell her, "Don't question, just enjoy." It took me about three days to figure out the perfect recipe for garlic frog legs, and I made a lot of mistakes along the way.

Believe it or not, after I'd mastered the recipe, I pulled the meat off the legs and turned it into frog soup. I was just thinking, "I have those frog legs left over, they have a great flavor, what could I do now?" Pull all the meat off, make a great roux, and just throw them in. Plus, I never like any meat to go to waste. That's the really crazy thing about life: you often start out intending to do one thing but end up doing something entirely different.

When Korie and I moved back to West Monroe, Louisiana, and I finished college at Northeast Louisiana University, I had no intention of going to work for Duck Commander. I liked to duck-hunt but wasn't into it as much as Phil, Jase, or Uncle Si, and I wanted to go out and make a name for myself doing something on my own. I enjoyed working at Camp Ch-Yo-Ca and really liked being around kids, and I was also working at White's Ferry Road Church as a youth minister. I loved the freedom working at the camp gave me to create and grow. And watching kids' lives change for the better was pretty satisfying. But before too long, Korie and I had a house full of our own kids. After our oldest son, John Luke, was born in October 1995, our oldest daughter, Sadie, came along in June 1997. Then we adopted little Will in December 2001, and Bella, our baby girl, was born in September 2002.

Working at Camp Ch-Yo-Ca was a lot of fun, but it was a nonprofit, so there wasn't much room for financial growth. And with four kids to feed, I realized I probably needed to find another job where I could eventually bring home a little more bacon. I never really thought about making a lot of money—

didn't really care, to be honest. I guess I always thought we should do it in reverse. Rather than go out and try to kill myself on a career while I was young and my kids were little, I wanted to be home with them more during that critical time. Then later, when they got older, I'd go out and try to do a little better for us. Korie and I didn't have a ton of money, but we were happy, and we never let the balance of our bank account dictate our happiness. I learned a lot running Camp Ch-Yo-Ca and felt like I made a sizable contribution, but I came to a point in my life when I knew it was time to make a change. Duck Commander was starting to get bigger, so I went to Phil and asked him about working there.

> RATHER THAN GO OUT AND TRY TO KILL MYSELF ON A CAREER WHILE I WAS YOUNG AND MY KIDS WERE LITTLE, I WANTED TO BE HOME WITH THEM MORE DURING THAT CRITICAL TIME.

"Oh yeah, come on board," Phil told me.

"What am I going to do?" I asked him.

"We'll figure something out," Phil said.

He never even asked how much I made or needed to make. You gotta love Phil.

I ended up cleaning the yard at Phil and Kay's house for about six months. I was just trying to learn as much as I could about the business, and Phil and Kay would give me little projects like constructing outbuildings and things like that. I poured concrete pathways between the buildings and tried to improve the work environment in the little ways I could. Kay was stoked to have someone do her "pet" projects that she had been wanting since we were kids. And the fact that she had one of her sons doing it was even better. But I had a college degree, so I wanted to put it to use and be more involved in the business side of Duck Commander. At the time, we were making hunting DVDs, selling about ten thousand of them a year. More and more people were catching on to Duck Commander, and I thought we should start trying to take advantage of the exposure and popularity.

"Dad, I need to talk to people," I told Phil. "I need to talk to our customers. I need to know what they're thinking, what they're buying, why they're buying this, and why they're buying that." We didn't have much money, so there was no marketing budget to speak of, which meant I needed to do it cheaply. We only talked to our customers when we went to shows around the country.

About that time, websites were getting more and more commonplace. I remember watching TV and every advertisement seemed to include a website address, where customers could go to learn more about the company and its products. I went to Phil and told him we needed a website, even though I really didn't know how to get to one. By that time, Duck Commander was using the Internet for some of its business dealings, but down at Phil and Kay's house, where the business was being run, the Internet access was spotty at best. It was, and still is, only accessible through satellite, and if it rained hard, you could forget it.

"If a man wants a duck call, he can pick up the phone and call me," Phil told me.

Korie: Phil told Willie he needed to go talk to my dad, Johnny, because he owned the website URL for Duck Commander, DuckCommander.com. Daddy had a background in publishing and realized pretty early that the Internet was eventually going to become the way in which companies sold their products to consumers. So he asked Phil if he ever intended to build a website, and Phil, of course, told him no. Over the years, Dad had helped Phil and Kay with the legal aspects of Duck Commander, like helping them file for patents and trademarks and borrowing money from the bank. Because Duck Commander was so seasonal—the company did really well during hunting season but sold very little during the summer—Phil and Kay sometimes borrowed money from my dad to get them through the slow times. Daddy always believed in Phil's company and his products and felt they had a good thing going.

So Dad worked out a deal with Phil and Kay. They agreed to let him launch DuckCommander.com and would give him products like duck calls and DVDs to sell on the site as payment for the money they owed. Daddy sold them until he'd made enough money for Phil and Kay to pay him back, and then he started buying the products directly from them to sell on the website. Dad rented mailing lists, printed catalogs, and mailed them all over the country. He even launched the first

Duck Commander TV commercial in an area of California that was really big into duck hunting. The first commercial showed Phil, Jase, and Si shooting ducks in slow motion at pretty close range, and Dad received a bunch of angry e-mails from animal rights activists. It didn't take them long to get over it, though. And he sold even more DVDs.

When Willie decided he wanted to get more involved with Duck Commander, he went to Dad to ask him to sell Duck Commander's website and mail-order business to us. We paid Daddy a down payment on it and then paid him a percentage of the sales until we paid him back what it was worth when we bought it. Willie and I ran the website out of our house. At the time, I'd been working as the children's minister at our church, so I left that job and ran the website from home while raising our children. Every night, I would wake up to feed Will or Bella a bottle and sit at the computer answering e-mails and filling orders. Every customer received a personalized e-mail from Willie or me.

> I WOULD WAKE UP TO FEED WILL OR BELLA A BOTTLE AND SIT AT THE COMPUTER ANSWERING E-MAILS AND FILLING ORDERS.

I was taking full advantage of being Phil Robertson's son. People would always e-mail me back and ask, "Are you really his son?" Phil had started this club called Duckaholics Anonymous, and it was like a twelve-step program for serious duck hunters. It was a great idea, but Phil kind of let it fizzle out.

We relaunched Duckaholics Anonymous and sold member-
ships to the club through the website. We'd send them news-
letters, giveaways, and things to get them even more involved
in Duck Commander. I would always answer the Duckaholics Anonymous members' e-mails first, and we'd talk to them
through the website. We tried to make the membership super
exclusive. This was before Facebook, but we decided we really
needed to be more interactive, so we'd publish a quote of the
day or something fun like that, kind of like we do on Facebook
now. This was also the time when Phil began doing a lot of
speaking. He had spoken at a few church men's events and the
word was spreading. He got invited to speak all over the country. So we began posting those dates on our website so people
could go hear him.

Korie: We paid a company about $25,000 to completely
overhaul the website. The new site included message boards,
forums, and a complete online retail store. People would call
the phone number on the site and thought they were calling
a warehouse, but they were actually calling our house! We'd
get phone calls at two o'clock in the morning from someone
in California who wanted a duck call or T-shirt. We'd just wake
up and take their orders. Daddy had put together an exten-
sive mailing list of customers who had bought from him in the
past, so Willie and I made up some postcards and sent them
to about thirty thousand people around the country telling
them to come visit our new site. Willie and I had some money

that we'd saved, but we were going into quite a bit of debt to make all of this happen. It was a risk, but one we knew we had to take.

I got a phone call from the post office one day, telling me I needed to come and pick up several thousand postcards that had been returned because of bad addresses. I didn't even know how that worked. I found out that you have to pay for the ones coming back to you, but it was the only way at the time to clean up your list and know which ones were good and which ones weren't. I went to the post office to pick them up and there were boxes and boxes of them. I loaded up my old

> I LET THE ACCIDENT INSPIRE ME AND REALIZED THE LORD LET ME LIVE FOR A PURPOSE.

Chevy Suburban and headed back to the house. Wouldn't you know it? I pulled out in front of a car and it T-boned me just as I left the post office. I had a sick cut on my head, and the postcards went flying everywhere. There were pictures of Phil with the web address DuckCommander

.com all over Highway 34 in Ouachita Parish. Some of them were even stuck to my head! Fortunately, I wasn't seriously hurt, and the other people in the car were fine. We did end up getting sued by four people—which was odd, because there were only three passengers in the car that hit me! I could have easily died that day. I let the accident inspire me and realized the Lord let me live for a purpose. It was a reminder of sorts— "Life is short, son; make it count." The wreck was my fault, no doubt, but I survived, and not everyone walks out of a vehicle after getting hit by another car at seventy miles per hour.

Korie: When the hunting DVDs came out every June, it was always a busy time. We would take preorders for the DVDs, and Willie and I would go to Office Depot and buy bubble envelopes and write every address by hand. While we were waiting for the DVDs to be finished, the envelopes would be scattered around our house, and we were trying to keep the kids out of them the entire time. Alan's oldest daughter, Anna, had graduated from high school by this time and started working for us, helping package orders. She would get to our house in the morning and I would hand her a stack of orders I had printed out late the night before. I don't know what I would have done without her. About this same time, Willie had started making a lot of trips with Phil to his speaking engagements. Willie would set up a booth wherever Phil was speaking, selling DVDs, hats, T-shirts, and other Duck Commander memorabilia. This further confirmed to Willie just how popular Duck Commander was becoming, and he began to realize that the company was capable of doing so much more.

At the bigger hunting shows I attended with Phil, I started talking to other companies about sponsoring our hunting DVDs. We already had some corporate sponsors, like Browning and Mossy Oak, but they weren't paying us a lot of money. Realtree, which produces the world's most popular camouflage, decided it wanted to get more involved in the waterfowl industry. In one of their planning meetings, Michael Waddell (who worked for them at the time) suggested they do that by partnering with Duck Commander. Most of the folks in the meeting seemed to shrug it off and thought there was no way to get the Duck Commander guys. We had been with Mossy Oak for a long time, and they thought even trying to get us would be fruitless. But one of the guys there that day thought he would give it a shot and contact Duck Commander. He went to—what else!—the website to get the phone number to call us. That was Brad Schorr. Brad had just started working for Realtree and had been a fan of Duck Commander for a long time. To him, it seemed like a natural fit and was certainly worth a try. Brad was trying to make a name in the company and knew this could be just the thing to do that.

Brad called the house one day and left a message with Korie for me to call him. Korie didn't give me the message.

Korie: Oops, I obviously didn't realize the importance of this call. With four babies to feed and everything else we were juggling at the time, I'm sure this wasn't the only thing I forgot. Thankfully, Romans 8:28 assures us, "And we know that in all things God works for the good of those who love Him, who have been called according to His purpose." Even in those times that we drop the ball.

Fortunately, Brad called back a week later and this time Korie gave me the message. Realtree was interested in sponsoring us. I was excited. I called Brad and we talked for like three hours. I was like a sponge soaking up all of the knowledge I could. I knew we were going to have to make some big moves to take our company to the next level and this was just the kind of change that I was ready to make.

I headed down to Phil's to talk it over. Phil was open to the idea but was worried about what our fans would think. Realtree was tied in with Benelli Shotguns, so a move to Realtree was going to also mean a move to Benelli. Phil had grown up shooting Browning shotguns and Browning had been good to us. Browning had produced a line of limited-edition Duck Commander gear and used Phil's image for their marketing campaign at one point, but that relationship had started to decline. All of the people that we had relationships with at Browning had recently lost their jobs or moved on for one reason or another, and we found ourselves without the connection that might have compelled us to stay. We knew that Benelli made an excellent gun, and Phil was intrigued and eager to try it out. After much discussion, it was decided that the time was right and it was the correct move to make. Jase was not so sure but in the end agreed to go along. So, we made the big switch to Realtree and Benelli Shotguns in 2005. It was right in the middle of hunting season, and I was making my first big move in the hunting industry. The decision served as a statement that Willie Robertson was here and Duck Commander was gonna do things differently.

It wasn't long before several other big sponsors came along. Federal Premium Ammunition was next. Federal became a huge partner for us, eventually putting Phil's face on their boxes of Black Cloud shells. That deal was made over a drink one night in Las Vegas. Federal had a new technology called flight stopper and was about to launch some new pellets that had never been used in shells at the time. They mixed the new pellets with standard pellets in a shell, which produced a tighter pattern that increased a gun's range. I knew putting us with this new technology would be a great fit. I told Kyle Tengwall, Federal's director of marketing at the time (he is now the vice president of marketing), "You should put Phil's picture on the box." I didn't know at the time that the only other man who has had his face on a box of shotgun shells was John Wayne. I was just throwing it out there, and fortunately Kyle agreed. He and I have become good friends over the years doing a lot of good business together. This was just the beginning. We picked up several other sponsors as well. Soon, our business was growing, not just in sales, but also with a great deal more sponsorship dollars than we had ever had before.

THE DECISION SERVED AS A STATEMENT THAT WILLIE ROBERTSON WAS HERE AND DUCK COMMANDER WAS GONNA DO THINGS DIFFERENTLY.

It was an exciting time. Phil was pretty pumped. "You're the man! That's what I'm talking about!" he said, telling everyone at Duck Commander, "Will was right about making the switch." Even though Phil started Duck Commander and is considered a legend by duck hunters everywhere, he was really never comfortable in the role of CEO. Phil was always kind of an enigma in the hunting industry. When he went to SHOT Show and the other big hunting conventions, he kind of kept to himself, and let's face it, he doesn't exactly look like the kind of guy people are comfortable just walking up to and striking up a conversation with. For Phil, the hunting shows were an opportunity to walk in, sell the products, and leave. All of the other hunting companies knew Duck Commander had a cult following from the hunting DVDs, but they wondered if Phil was a little too dangerous to touch. He was kind of rogue and did things that everyone else was afraid to try. In fact, none of us were stereotypical duck hunters; we're not the white-collar guys who dress up in camo on the weekends and go hunting.

> THE OTHER HUNTING COMPANIES KNEW DUCK COMMANDER HAD A CULT FOLLOWING FROM THE HUNTING DVDs, BUT THEY WONDERED IF PHIL WAS A LITTLE TOO DANGEROUS.

Korie: Duck Commander was well-known in the hunting industry and had a strong group of loyal fans, but no man is an island, and neither is any good company. Phil wasn't the kind of guy to network at the industry shows and events. But Willie has enough of Kay's social gene in him to get the job done. He enjoys meeting new people. Willie feels like there is something he can learn from everyone he meets, and you never really know when a new relationship will be an important one in business or a good friend down the road. When Willie started meeting with these other companies, they realized the

Duckmen were not as scary as they had once believed. One of the executives said Willie "looked like them, but thinks like us." Willie had the beard and camo like Phil and Jase, but he had a mind that could connect the dots with the business end of things. Willie always told the executives he met with, "You know what? We are what we are, but we have a really good reputation. We're a family-owned operation, and we've always done things the right way. We don't make excuses for who we are." And lots of companies got it and were excited to jump on board.

By the time I came back to work at Duck Commander, Al had gone to seminary and become a preacher and Jase had become a really big part of the operation, making the duck calls and appearing on the DVDs with Phil. We know that if something ever happens to Phil, Jase will be right there to continue his legacy. Jase is second in command in the duck blind and, like Phil, knows how to make a duck call sound just like a duck. Jase and Phil love to hunt and they love being in the blind more than anywhere else. It's almost like Phil's personality is split right down the middle between Jase and me. Jase got Phil's passion for duck hunting and I got his entrepreneurial spirit. So even though Jase and I don't agree all the time, when it comes to Duck Commander, we make the perfect team. Each of us brings his own unique set of skills to the table without stepping on the other's toes in the process. We each do what we were born to do and what we truly love. I don't think it gets any better than that.

Even though things were starting to pick up for Duck Commander, the company was still a mess financially. In the early days of Duck Commander, Phil made the duck calls and DVDs, and Kay ran the business. It got to be too much for only Phil and Kay to handle, so Jase, and eventually his wife, Missy, began taking on more and more, but he never enjoyed the business side of the company. Jase somewhat reluctantly began making sales calls to Walmart and some other big customers, but even he'll tell you he never really had a passion for it. Kay was overwhelmed with the bookkeeping, accounting, and payroll. She was doing the best she could, but it was really just too big a job for her. She was feeling stretched physically and mentally and was even having stomach ulcers because she was so stressed out. Even though sales were picking up, Duck Commander was still only a seasonal business. We did really well during hunting season, but after hunting season ended, it was a struggle to keep our doors open. Kay was out of her league when the business started actually growing. It is hard to keep up with inventory, payroll, employees, and everything else. She was about ready to cash it in.

To help make ends meet during the summer, Kay gave some of our local customers huge discounts. If a retailer called and ordered products for the next hunting season, Kay would offer them a big discount if they paid for their products in advance. That's how badly Duck Commander needed cash flow during the summer. In the end, we would end up losing money on those products, but it was the only way Kay could keep the business going during the slow times.

Finally, after working at the company for several months, I went to Kay and Phil and told them I wanted to take over the business operations of Duck Commander. Kay was more than happy to turn them over to me because she was completely overwhelmed. But I told them I had to have complete authority to do what I needed to do. Korie and I talked about it for a long time and decided to buy half of Duck Commander from my parents. We took out a second mortgage on our house to buy half of the company. Duck Commander really needed a cash investment at the time, and Kay and Phil had stretched their borrowing power to its limit. I told them, "If I'm going to do it, then I'm going to do it."

Korie: When Willie and I bought half of Duck Commander, we knew we were taking a leap of faith. There were definitely some obstacles we were going to have to overcome, but we believed in what Phil and Kay started and wanted more than anything to see it reach its full potential. Phil and Kay were super supportive. In a lot of companies, when control is passed from one generation to the next, the older generation has a hard time letting go and is somewhat resistant to any kind of change. Phil and Kay weren't that way at all. In fact, they were completely the opposite. They gave Willie all the respect and room he needed to learn and grow. Willie gave them just

WE BELIEVED IN WHAT PHIL AND KAY STARTED AND WANTED MORE THAN ANYTHING TO SEE IT REACH ITS FULL POTENTIAL.

as much respect in return, asking Phil and Kay for advice and suggestions when needed. The transition ended up being seamless.

After I took over the business operations of Duck Commander, one of the first big decisions I made was to get us more involved in retail stores like Gander Mountain, Cabela's, Academy Sports and Outdoors, Dick's Sporting Goods, and Bass Pro Shops, as well as the huge independent stores like Mack's Prairie Wings and Simmons Sporting Goods. We had been doing business with them for a while by that time, but I knew it needed to be more of our focus. Those stores were in the hunting business three hundred and sixty-five days a year. For several years, Walmart was about 80 percent of our business. It was great having our products in Walmart, but it was always a tricky situation. Walmart stocked hunting products during hunting season and then replaced them with something else when hunting season was over. You'd go meet one of Walmart's buyers and expect to get eight dollars for a duck call. But then the buyer would tell you he wasn't paying more than four dollars. Now, nobody wanted to come home and tell everyone that he'd lost the Walmart account, especially when it was such a huge percentage of our business. It was always a big day around the Robertson house when Walmart wired its money to our account to pay for its products. But by the time you shipped the products the way Walmart wanted them shipped, you really weren't making much money. Those big checks that came in always seemed to get spent before we knew it, because there wasn't much profit in them, which created a big cycle of debt for several years.

I wanted to make sure Duck Commander would be okay if anything ever happened to the Walmart account. So we invested in our relationships with the year-round hunting stores, which became a big part of our business. Wouldn't you know it? Within two years, Walmart decided it was getting out of the waterfowl market altogether. Typically, a setback like that will kill a company. Fortunately, we had a contingency plan and were able to survive without Walmart for a few years. I'm happy to say, though, that in the last two years, Walmart began stocking our duck calls and other products again, and it has become a mutually beneficial relationship once again.

After Walmart stopped buying from us that year, I went three months without being able to cash my own paycheck. Korie and I had to rein in our spending. I told her, "Don't buy anything unless it's absolutely necessary." We were living on a tight budget. I knew I needed to get Duck Commander on an even tighter budget till I could find another source of revenue to keep the company afloat. Duck Commander was like a batch of frog legs sitting in the fridge waiting for you to figure out how you were going to cook them. The hard-

DUCK COMMANDER WAS LIKE A BATCH OF FROG LEGS SITTING IN THE FRIDGE WAITING FOR YOU TO FIGURE OUT HOW YOU WERE GOING TO COOK THEM.

est part of having frog legs for dinner is catching the wild frogs and bringing them home. Then you have to clean them and get the meat ready to eat. Phil had done the hard part with Duck Commander. It was primed and ready to take off. All that was needed was a guy who could imagine what else it could be.

GARLIC FROG LEGS

I had some frogs and garlic and dreamed this up one night. It is so good. For the few hundred who will actually go get frogs, try it. The rest, well . . . use chicken instead. Good luck.

8–10 pounds of frog legs
1 can of beer
Phil Robertson's Zesty Cajun Style Seasoning
2 cups flour
1 stick butter
¼ cup garlic-infused grape-seed oil
2 cups white wine
bulb of garlic, cloves peeled
1 cup fresh mushrooms

1. Soak frog legs in beer for an hour or so. Drain.
2. Season frog legs with Zesty Cajun Style Seasoning.
3. Roll frog legs in flour and set aside.
4. In a large black skillet bring butter and grape-seed oil up to high (don't burn the butter; it will brown when burning). It doesn't take much oil and butter, just about a half inch or so.
5. When oil and butter starts sizzling, put frog legs in and brown on each side. The oil-and-butter mixture should be about half-way up the legs, just enough to brown them.
6. If butter gets low, throw another half stick in. Set browned frog legs aside.
7. With what's left in the pan, add white wine, garlic, and mushrooms, and cook for 3 to 4 minutes.
8. Add frog legs to white wine mix. Cover and simmer for 30 minutes until meat is falling off bone. (You will know it's done, believe me!)

11

CHICKEN FEET

PRAISE BE TO THE GOD AND FATHER OF OUR LORD JESUS
CHRIST, WHO HAS BLESSED US IN THE HEAVENLY REALMS
WITH EVERY SPIRITUAL BLESSING IN CHRIST. FOR HE CHOSE
US IN HIM BEFORE THE CREATION OF THE WORLD TO BE HOLY
AND BLAMELESS IN HIS SIGHT. IN LOVE HE PREDESTINED
US FOR ADOPTION TO SONSHIP THROUGH JESUS CHRIST,
IN ACCORDANCE WITH HIS PLEASURE AND WILL.
—EPHESIANS 1:3–5

Korie: When I was a student at Ouachita Christian School, my senior-year Bible teacher, David Matthews, adopted a little five-year-old boy. In class that year, we talked a lot about how important it was for Christians families to adopt and that children should never be left without a home and loving parents. The idea always stuck with me. James 1:27 says: "Religion that God our Father accepts as pure and faultless is this: to look after orphans and widows in their distress and to keep oneself from being polluted by the world."

When we were dating, like most couples, Willie and I talked about how many kids we wanted to have. I told Willie about my desire to adopt and he was all for it. We both grew up with big families so we decided we wanted to have four kids, with at least one of them through adoption. We never knew how that would happen. We didn't know if we would adopt a boy or a girl or a newborn baby or older child. We decided we would remain open, and if God wanted it to happen, it would happen.

There were several families at White's Ferry Road Church that adopted children, including one couple that had adopted biracial twins. Their lawyer came to them and asked if they were interested in adopting another biracial child who was about to be born. They told her they couldn't do it at the time, but they remembered that we had expressed an interest in adopting a child. Their lawyer called Willie and me and told us how difficult it was to place biracial children in homes in the South. We were shocked. It was the twenty-first century. We committed to being a part of changing that in our society. Skin color should not make a difference.

We told the lawyer we were definitely interested, and we started to go through the process of adopting the baby in 2000. We began paying for the mother's living expenses and medical bills, and Willie and I were really getting excited about bringing another child into our home. Our oldest son, John Luke, was almost five, and Sadie, our daughter, was three. We thought it was the perfect time to bring another baby into our home. But then we found out the mother had promised the baby to a few other families, who were also paying her expenses. The woman had nine children, some of which she had kept and others she had given up for adoption. The lawyer told us we needed to step away from the situation. We were absolutely devastated and heartbroken. It was such a roller-coaster ride and so emotional and traumatic. Willie and I decided we still wanted to adopt a child, but we weren't going to force the issue. Maybe it just wasn't in God's plan for us right then.

WE STARTED TO GO THROUGH THE PROCESS OF ADOPTING THE BABY IN 2000.

After we lost the child, Willie and I decided we would have another baby naturally and then maybe adopt a fourth child a few years later. I had gotten pregnant very easily with John Luke and Sadie. Well, nine months went by and I still wasn't pregnant. I wasn't really worried about it, but it seemed a little strange since I'd gotten pregnant so easily the first two times.

We had a friend who was teaching birthing classes at a children's home. The class was for pregnant teenagers, some of whom were putting their babies up for adoption. She knew we were still interested in adoption, so she asked us if we were ready. We filled out the paperwork and only a couple of weeks later, the adoption agency called us and told us it had a couple of babies available. There was a boy who was already born and a girl who was about to be born. The director showed us a picture of the boy and we fell in love instantly! He was beautiful, a perfectly healthy eight-pound, two-ounce bundle of joy. We felt like he was ours from the moment we saw him and couldn't wait to get him in our hands. We rushed through the adoption process. The adoption agency came out and did three days of home studies with us, and then we went and picked him up the very next week. It was that fast. Willie and I felt extremely blessed and thankful for this precious baby boy who was now ours and were confident that this was God's plan for our life and for this little boy's life all along.

We made a nursery in our house and set up a crib, and our son Willie Alexander Robertson came to our home when he was five weeks old in mid-December 2001. We named him after Willie, of course, and his middle name came from his papaw Phil, whose middle name is Alexander. Little Will didn't even weigh nine pounds when we got him and was just so happy and sweet. He had been living with a foster family who took excellent care of him. We went down to Baton Rouge, Louisiana, and picked him up. Then we returned home to a house full of friends and family, who had made a huge WELCOME HOME WILL sign and showered us with gifts and love. Will was just perfect and precious, and I have enjoyed every minute of mothering him. We are forever grateful to Will's birth mother, who loved him enough to give him the life she knew he deserved.

In the meantime, I still wasn't taking birth control. It all happened so fast, and I was too busy making bottles and changing diapers to think about it. For our tenth wedding

> WILLIE ALEXANDER ROBERTSON CAME TO OUR HOME WHEN HE WAS FIVE WEEKS OLD IN MID-DECEMBER 2001.

anniversary in January 2002, Willie surprised me with a trip to Cancún, Mexico. We drove to Dallas, and I thought we were just going to spend a few days there. Always the romantic, Willie didn't tell me we were going to Mexico until he handed me a note at the airport! It was an awesome surprise, but I was a little reluctant leaving our two-month-old baby at home. Thankfully, my mom was in on the surprise and was fully prepared for and capable of caring for the three little ones we had left with her and my dad. Willie and I had an awesome time in Cancún—it was the first real trip we had had since having kids—and we enjoyed it to its fullest. We came home refreshed and renewed and thankful for our life together.

Needless to say, I was a little shocked about a month later when I found out I was pregnant, but with that news we were even more certain of God's plan for our life. God had closed my womb until Will was in our home, and then opened it to give us our fourth child. Our baby girl, Bella Chrysanne, was born in September 2002. So that's how we came to have two babies just ten months apart.

I'd be lying if I didn't admit that things were nuts there for a while. And I can promise you, while I helped in the discipline department, it's Korie who gets all the credit for doing the hard work. She is an incredible mom and has always taken the role of motherhood very seriously. I don't know how she did it all, but she did, usually with a baby on each hip. This was also my motivation to start being good at business, so I could provide enough money for all these younguns. Let me tell you something: KIDS AIN'T CHEAP. Doctor bills, food, Pampers, and all that other stuff cost money, and I committed to go and push myself further to bring home more bacon, and a lot more cabbage, as in cash.

I'D BE LYING IF I DIDN'T ADMIT THAT THINGS WERE NUTS THERE FOR A WHILE.

It's amazing how when you have four children, you get four different personalities. You would think that when you raise kids the same way in the same home with the same values, they should all turn out the same, right? Wrong. God made every child special, with a unique personality and temperament, fears and hopes, likes and dislikes. And aren't we glad He didn't make us all the same? Life is just so much more interesting that way. Not to mention challenging.

Korie: John Luke and Sadie had their own unique challenges. John Luke was hospitalized with RSV (respiratory syncytial virus, which causes respiratory tract infections) when he was three months old and it seemed to damage his lungs, so we spent a lot of time at the doctor's office with wheezing, bronchitis, and pneumonia, but other than that, he was an easy, fun kid to raise. He loved to read, just like I do, so we spent hours reading books, and he seemed to love to learn about everything. He was also a climber who loved the outdoors. He loved animals so much so that at one point we weren't sure if he would follow in the family hunting tradition. He had every kind of animal, from goats to rabbits, to snakes, to leopard geckos, to an iguana.

One time, when he was about six years old, he and Willie

found a bat down at the camp that for some reason they decided they were going to nurse back to health. We set up a little cage for the bat on our back porch and warned John Luke not to touch him. He begged and begged to touch the bat, and one day decided that he would not really be touching him if he put on gloves first. So he put on some of my yellow rubber kitchen gloves and without my knowing tried to pick up the bat! Of course, the bat bit him on his little finger. He came and told me what he had done and showed me. Sure enough, there were two little bite marks on his finger. I immediately Googled what you do for bat bites and found out that bats are highly likely to carry rabies! We rushed John Luke to the hospital. They gave him the first round of rabies shots just in case and said that they would have to test the bat. If the bat tested positive for rabies, then John Luke would have to go through about five rounds of shots. The doctor asked if we still had the bat and said that we had

THAT'S WHEN JOHN LUKE STARTED CRYING. "HE DOESN'T HAVE RABIES, I KNOW HE DOESN'T. IT'S NOT THE BAT'S FAULT!"

to turn it in to have it tested for rabies. That's when John Luke started crying. "He doesn't have rabies, I know he doesn't. It's not the bat's fault!" he cried. He was devastated that they had to kill the bat to test him because of something he had done. John Luke said that he would get the shots so that the bat wouldn't have to be tested. This was huge. John Luke hated shots and still does, but he was willing to get more if he could only save the bat.

As John Luke got older and started hunting with Willie, he took to it naturally. I guess it's in his blood, as they say. The first time John Luke killed a deer, he was so proud to be able to feed our family. We ate on it for weeks. He was becoming a man and fully understood the circle of life. I'm so proud of the young man he has become. He is a leader at his school and at our church and an incredible big brother to his younger siblings.

Our daughter Sadie Carroway was as healthy as she could be. I had her in the summer when Camp Ch-Yo-Ca's sessions were in full swing. Her delivery was easy, and I was at the camp with her when she was only a few days old. The kids passed her around and loved on her. I was a young mom and didn't worry a bit about germs. Maybe that's why she never gets sick: she was exposed to everything with all those little hands touching her as a baby, and she developed immunities. Who knows? She was like the little camp mascot. She was a happy baby who reached for her bed when she was tired. But she seemed to have a stronger spirit than John Luke. We could tell from an early age that she was going to be a competitive little one. She loves sports and had a baseball birthday party at two years old! She's got a lot of her daddy in her. She loves to entertain and make people laugh.

When Sadie was only four years old, she was already doing impersonations of all the family members—just like her dad. She also went through a stage where she would preach. It was the cutest thing we had ever seen. We have a video of her preaching where she says, "It doesn't matter if you are a teacher or a stealer, a policeman or a jail person. God still loves you, and He wants you to be in heaven with Him. He doesn't want you to go down there with the devil. He loves you and He will forgive all your sins. All you have to do is ask Him. . . ." It goes on and on. She sings some songs, then she breaks into a cheer. "Let's give it up for God!" she shouts. She had so much wisdom for such a little one. Willie nicknamed her "the Original" from the time she could talk. It fits her perfectly.

WHEN SADIE WAS ONLY FOUR YEARS OLD, SHE WAS ALREADY DOING IMPERSONATIONS OF ALL THE FAMILY MEMBERS—JUST LIKE HER DAD.

Then came Will and Bella. These two little ones who had come into our life around the same time were quite the handful! Will was a very happy baby. He would literally wake up laughing. We loved to listen to him talking to himself in his bed for a while when he first woke up. He was a very easy baby; then he became a very busy toddler!

Bella wasn't so easy as a baby but is the most fun child one could ever have. She contracted salmonella when she was only three weeks old. It was terrifying! We never found out for sure how she got it. There were some other cases of salmonella from formula that had been reported, but we had also picked up a turtle on the side of the road coming home from church that day. Turtles can sometimes carry salmonella. She, of course, didn't touch the turtle, but one of us could have touched it and then passed it to her. We just weren't sure. Anyway, I was holding her that night when all of a sudden she felt warm. A three-week-old baby should never have a fever.

I knew immediately something was wrong. We rushed her to the hospital. They didn't know what was wrong with her, so they did a spinal tap to make sure she didn't have meningitis. It was horrible to see our little baby go through that ordeal. By the next morning she was having severe diarrhea. It took several days before they figured out exactly what was wrong with her and gave her antibiotics she needed to make her better. She was so sick and was in the hospital for about a week. She lost weight and was the tiniest little thing, but eventually made a full recovery and we were very thankful!

Poor thing, though, she had stomach trouble for about a year after this. She just couldn't hold down anything. I had to feed her every three hours, even through the night, until she was about nine months old, just to try to put some meat on her bones. She cried so much she was perpetually hoarse. But she was the most beautiful little thing and had the most confident little spirit. She started walking at nine months old. Those little toothpick legs didn't look like they could hold her up, but they did, and once she started walking, she was off.

Like I said, the babies were only ten months apart, so Will wasn't even walking when Bella was born. But once they both started walking, there was no stopping them. We called them Destructo 1 and Destructo 2. I used to tell people that one would raise the window and the other would climb out. This was our life for a while. I couldn't keep my eyes on them enough to keep them out of trouble. Bella seemed to have a perpetual knot on her head and our house was always a wreck. If Will and Bella were left alone for any length of time, I can promise you something was going to be destroyed. They would squeeze the toothpaste out of the tube and smear it all over the bathroom mirror, get into the pantry and dump all the cereal out of the boxes—and this was all before eight A.M.!

ONCE WILL AND BELLA STARTED WALKING, THERE WAS NO STOPPING THEM. WE CALLED THEM DESTRUCTO 1 AND DESTRUCTO 2.

We could not take those two any-where. They were born with the full con-fidence that they knew exactly where they were going when their legs hit the floor, and they were off. I couldn't keep up with them. I never put them on a leash, but I probably should have. I carried them as much as I could, one on each hip. People would say, "How do you do that?" I told them it was better than the alternative; if I put them down, they would both go in different directions and it was all over. Keeping them on my hip was the only way I could stay in control. Once they got too big for me to carry, I would make them hold my hand. They would try so hard to squirm out of my hand, but I would just squeeze and make them hang on.

Korie says that once she could tell all the kids, "Go brush your teeth and put your PJs on," and they could actually do it by themselves, she knew we would survive! For a while there, she was so consumed with babies that I don't know how she did anything else. But she did. We would end up most nights with at least three of the four kids in our bed. Our rule was that none of the kids could start out in the bed with us, but if they woke up in the night, they could come get in our bed. This was very different than when I was growing up. We would have never climbed in bed with our parents. Phil was not the snuggling type. But it was fun waking up to all the love and laughter, even if our backs suffered for it. Our babies were growing along with the Duck Commander business and our website, and I was starting to do some traveling with Dad for his speaking engagements. It was busy, but it was fun! I loved watching the kids change and grow into their own unique little people.

Korie: We have one more daughter who came to us from a unique place. Growing up, our family traveled a lot and I always thought it was important for kids to experience different cultures and learn from people who grew up differently than them. Of course, it's tough to travel with four little ones, so I thought I would bring someone to us. We decided to take in an exchange student. I didn't know at the time she would become such an awesome big sister to our kids and we would become her American family forever and always.

Rebecca Ann Lo joined our family when she was sixteen years old. She came as an exchange student from Taiwan and must have wondered what she'd gotten herself into joining a family of bearded men who hunted for a living. She was the youngest of four in her family in Taiwan, but when she joined our home, she became the oldest. Also, she lost her father at a young age and I think having a strong father figure in Willie really helped her growth. Our kids were young when Rebecca joined us in the summer of 2004, and they were so excited to welcome her into our family. We made signs welcoming her to America, and when she stepped off the plane, the kids could barely contain their excitement. Will hid behind a chair because he just didn't know what to do. Bella went up and held her hand, and John Luke and Sadie started talking a hundred miles an hour.

REBECCA ANN LO JOINED OUR FAMILY WHEN SHE WAS SIXTEEN YEARS OLD. SHE CAME AS AN EXCHANGE STUDENT FROM TAIWAN.

They had a new playmate and were eager to tell her everything there was to know about our family. We quickly realized she couldn't understand a word we said!

She had learned some English in school in Taiwan, but with our Southern accents, Rebecca just could not understand us. Somehow she and I figured out how to communicate, and we bonded. She stuck to me like glue for a while. If someone asked her a question, she would look to me to answer. I read her children's books at night and taught her English through reading the menus at restaurants! I remember the first day I took her to school; I literally had to pry her fingers off my arm. It was like having another kindergartener. She was scared to death. But by the end of the school year, she was speaking English well, with even a little bit of a Louisianan accent. And we fell in love with her and didn't want her to leave. We told her that if she wanted to come back for her senior year, she was more than welcome. Her mom said no at first. She had, of course, missed her daughter and wanted her to come home. But a few weeks before the next school year started, Rebecca called and said excitedly, "Mom said I can come!" She booked her plane ticket back to Louisiana and has been here ever since.

When Rebecca came to live with us, everybody thought I looked like Johnny Damon, an outfielder with the Boston Red Sox, who had a big ol' beard. Korie's dad, Johnny, even gave me a life-size cutout of Damon, which I kept in my office. Well, that entire first year that Rebecca lived with us, I told her I used to be a professional baseball player. She went to a party for foreign exchange students and told everyone that I was an ex–Major League Baseball player! She kept telling everyone, "Willie is very famous." She thought it was the coolest thing and even told her mother and sister I was famous. I finally broke the news to Rebecca that I wasn't really a baseball player. Fortunately, she still loved me anyway. I can only imagine her family's surprise when they went on the Internet and found out whom she was really living with!

After Duck Commander signed a licensing deal with Weaver, which makes rifle and shotgun optical scopes, I wanted to tour their manufacturing center in Taiwan. We took Rebecca as our translator and toured Taiwan. I promised Rebecca I would eat something weird while I was there. I took a small bite of fried chicken feet, but there wasn't any meat. I'm not sure how the Taiwanese eat those. It's a chicken's foot.

I couldn't stomach eating the century egg, which is another Chinese tradition. They preserve duck, chicken, or quail eggs in a mixture of clay, ash, salt, lime, and rice hulls for several months. The egg yolk turns dark green and smells like ammonia. I've eaten some pretty crazy stuff in my life, but that wasn't one of them!

Rebecca's mom and sister came to visit us for a couple of weeks one time, and her mom cooked delicious Taiwanese food for us. Rebecca has been back to Taiwan a couple of times to visit her family there. But we are her American mom and dad. We are family. She graduated from Louisiana State University with a bachelor's degree in fashion design and merchandising, and we are so proud of everything she has accomplished. More important, we are proud of the beautiful Christian lady she has become and the great big sister she has been to our kids. We love her and are thankful God saw fit to place her in our home.

ARMADILLO EGGS

You didn't think I was going to give you a recipe for chicken feet, did you? I don't really know why these are called armadillo eggs, but they are, and they are tasty. This is a base for many dishes I make. Anything can be added to it at any time. I have used cherries, jams, candied jalapeños, real mozzarella slivers, and many different kinds of meat. If you're not sure it's done after grilling or broiling your bacon, put it in a black pot, add a little butter or olive oil over the top, cover for ten or fifteen minutes, and let steam.

6 to 8 whole jalapeños, sliced
1 package cream cheese
2 pounds breakfast sausage, formed into 6 to 8 patties
1 pound thin-sliced bacon
1 stick of butter, melted

1. Slice jalapeños in half lengthwise.
2. Use one half of each jalapeño for each armadillo egg. Scoop out seeds and veins and then fill each half with cream cheese.
3. Mold sausage patty around jalapeño, making sure to cover the entire jalapeño pepper.
4. Wrap each armadillo egg with a slice of bacon.
5. Cook "eggs" on open grill until bacon is crispy and sausage is thoroughly cooked, about ten to fifteen minutes.
6. Remove eggs from grill and cover with melted butter.

12

FAST FOOD

CHILDREN, OBEY YOUR PARENTS IN THE LORD, FOR THIS IS RIGHT. "HONOR YOUR FATHER AND MOTHER"—WHICH IS THE FIRST COMMANDMENT WITH A PROMISE—"SO THAT IT MAY GO WELL WITH YOU AND THAT YOU MAY ENJOY LONG LIFE ON THE EARTH."
—EPHESIANS 6:1–3

orie: After people watch *Duck Dynasty,* I often get comments on Twitter and from fans that I come into contact with about how well-mannered our kids are. In the South, traditionally children are expected to say "Yes, ma'am" and "No, sir" to adults. It's important for children to show respect for their elders, but I'm afraid that even in the South, that is something that is fading from our society. I'm really proud of our kids for the way they behave, the way they act toward adults, and their manners in general.

When the *Duck Dynasty* crew was here filming the scene where Phil had our kids clean up an area of his land to make a football field, I think the crew members expected our kids to be griping and complaining about having to do it. But our kids would never do that, at least not within earshot of their papaw Phil. Even if they didn't want to do it, they would never complain to their grandfather if he asked them to do something. That's not the way they were raised.

In the Robertson house, kids are expected to fit in with the family and do what the family does. Whenever I need the kids to do something, I always say, "All right, kids, it's family cleanup time," "family wash-the-car time," or "family clean-out-the-garage time." You get the idea. When I announce "family time," everyone is expected to join in. It's nonnegotiable, and you don't get paid for it. You just do it, because you are part of the family.

IN THE ROBERTSON HOUSE, KIDS ARE EXPECTED TO FIT IN WITH THE FAMILY AND DO WHAT THE FAMILY DOES.

Not that our kids don't have plenty of activities of their own. But sometimes when a family's life totally revolves around the kids, parents can start to feel like their children are a burden. We've never felt that way. Our lives didn't end when we brought children into the world. When our kids were younger, I just put them on my hip and took them with me wherever I went. If it meant they had to fall asleep on my shoulder while I was answering e-mails or filling orders, then that's just the way it would be. Kids only know what you teach them. If you let the whole world revolve around them when they are younger, when they realize that's not really the way the world works, it's not very pretty.

Having said all that, somebody told me once that they'd never seen anyone watch their children as much as we do. We'll sit around at night just watching them doing tricks and performing for us. That was something I brought from my side

of the family. My family absolutely loves to watch our kids perform. It's really one of our favorite things to do. I think enjoying your children and delighting in them is a gift that you give
your children. It's a way to show them that they are loved
and valued. Plus, there's nothing cuter than a three-year-old
showing off her latest dance moves.

Hey, wait a minute, I will never forget being in the eighth
grade and one Friday night telling Phil about "break dancing."
Phil said, "What's that?" I told him, "Let me show ya." I put
my boom box down, put in my cassette of Midnight Star's "No
Parking on the Dance Floor," and did an entire dance while
Phil watched from his recliner. He seemed impressed. "That's
some kinda moves, Will," he told me. "Not sure what that is,
but at least it's entertaining." So even the Robertson side did a
little watchin'!

Korie: Another thing we've always tried to teach our children is that people are more important than things. If one
of the kids is watching TV and somebody wants to talk, you
stop watching TV and listen to them. You
never put more importance on a thing
than you do on a person. This is hard
for older siblings to learn when there are
little ones in the family destroying your
favorite toys. But it was a lesson we
were intent on teaching. If you are going
to teach these tough lessons, though,

WE'VE ALWAYS
TRIED TO
TEACH OUR
CHILDREN THAT
PEOPLE ARE
ALWAYS MORE
IMPORTANT
THAN THINGS.

you have to model them in your own life. When your neighbor borrows your lawn mower and tears it up, you have to act with love and forgiveness. It's in the little things and the big things. Your children are always watching.

This was a hard lesson for me because I came from such a poor family. When I was a child, you really took pride in having any possessions. But Korie and her family could always go out and buy a replacement when something got lost or broke. She actually taught me a lot about this lesson in our early marriage days. I was used to protecting my stuff from my brothers like the Secret Service.

Korie: Willie and I have always thought that your home should be the happiest place for your family. If you're excited when your kids or husband walks in the front door, then you'll have a much happier family. A lot of people don't make it a habit to do that. They go to work and give their best to the outside world because they know if they're negative or griping or complaining, they might lose their job. They're not going to make a sale with a frown on their faces, so they're always putting on their best smile. It should be that way at home too. I always tell our children that the people they love the most and the people who love them the most are their family. So your family should be the people you treat the best.

When the kids come home every day, we really try to make it a point to greet them, be happy, and ask them how their days went. I do the same thing for Willie, and he does the same thing for me. When Willie comes home, I'm excited. I hug him and kiss him. We find out what happened in each other's day, and it sets the right tone for everything else. Our kids see our love for each other, and they realize that's how they should be treating one another too.

I think having happy kids and a happy marriage is all about respect. Willie and I have a mutual respect for each other, and we try to treat each other respectfully. Sadie once asked me why marriage is so hard. She realized married couples don't always make it and that there are a lot of people getting divorced. Our kids see that Willie and I are happy and think marriage looks pretty easy. Of course, they didn't see us during the early years, when times were tough. In those days we fought our way through all the things newlyweds have to figure out in order to live together peacefully. I told Sadie that sometimes it's hard because you go into a marriage with expectations, and you think the other person is going to be

HAVING HAPPY KIDS AND A HAPPY MARRIAGE IS ALL ABOUT RESPECT.

a certain way. You want them to be that way because that's how you always envisioned your husband or wife, or that's how your daddy or mama was when you were growing up. But until you can let those expectations go, and value your spouse for who he or she really is and be thankful for it, then a marriage is never going to work.

I'm very different from Willie's mom, and Willie is very different from my dad. So if you go into a marriage with all these unrealistic expectations and try to change your spouse to be exactly like you want them to be, then you're always going to be fighting and miserable. But if you can let those false expectations go, you can learn to appreciate and be thankful for who that person is, and then marriage can be a great thing.

I think marriages start to go bad when selfishness creeps in. Korie and I are super laid-back, in a lot of ways like my parents were. I never liked taking orders, never liked being bossed around, and I didn't marry a parent figure. There is no sense in my giving her orders or her giving me orders; we're both adults. I married somebody to share my life with. You have to let your spouse be the person they want to be, and you have to let them do the things they want to do. If she doesn't feel like cleaning the kitchen one day, she doesn't have to. If I feel it needs to be cleaned, I can do it myself, or hire someone to do it. I don't tell her what to do. I'm not her father. She does the same for me.

Korie ended up working at Duck Commander with me, but if she wanted to do something entirely different, I would have supported her. As the kids have gotten older and as the business has grown, there have been times where I've told her, "If you want to stop, you can stop. Don't feel like you have to work." I've asked her several times if she didn't want me to go on the road, and if she hadn't wanted me to go, I wouldn't have gone. Now, she'd have had to realize that the business might have suffered from it, but if it did, then so be it. Making a little extra money is never worth it if it's at the expense of your family. If you work with your spouse, then you really have to respect each other and communicate well. Those are the keys to living and working with your spouse happily.

Korie: When Willie was growing up, he always knew what the consequences were if he misbehaved or acted out of line, and it was the same in my home. We try to never yell at our kids or even raise our voices at them. I can honestly say that I have never heard Willie yell at our children but he has always disciplined them with an immediate action. I remember one time when the kids were fighting and driving me crazy. The TV was turned up really loud, and they were yelling at each other, fighting over some toy or what movie they were going to watch next. Willie came through the door and saw that I was about at my wit's end. He just walked over and turned the TV off. The kids looked at him and thought, "Wait, what just happened?" There was complete silence in the room. Without saying a word, Willie was telling them, "If you're going to fight, then you're not going to get to watch TV." The argument was over, and there was no discussion or arguing back and forth. Willie just put an end to it.

> THE ARGUMENT WAS OVER, AND THERE WAS NO DISCUSSION OR ARGUING BACK AND FORTH. WILLIE JUST PUT AN END TO IT.

That's how discipline generally works in our house. When our kids were toddlers, if one of our kids woke up from a nap and was whiny or in a bad mood, then he or she was expected to turn around and go straight back to his or her room. If one of the kids is driving everybody else crazy, then he or she is removed from the situation. They're sent to their room until they can get along with everyone else.

But Willie seems to get his point across better than me. I'm usually the one who wakes the kids up for school in the morning, and Bella takes forever to get out of bed. I have to admit, I was the same way for my mom, so maybe I have too much patience for it. But I have to roll her over and keep prodding her to get up. Then I have to go back and check to make sure she didn't go back to sleep after I left. But Willie literally just walks into a room and turns on a light. He says, "Get up," and they get up. I'm always like, "How in the world did you do that?" I guess that's just the difference between mamas and daddies, and it's important to have that balance.

When the kids are misbehaving, I don't count to three. One is enough. I try not to be the one always saying no, but when I do, it should carry some weight. I try to be the parent who disciplines our kids because I don't want Korie to be burdened with it. I think Korie and I have really defined roles in how we handle situations. Korie's tolerance line has always been a lot higher than mine. My kids will test me, but they understand that when they reach my tolerance line, that's it and it's over. The key is being consistent so you never confuse them.

I never raise my voice. Phil never yelled at us when I was growing up. When Phil said it, he said it and didn't have to scream. I see people yelling at their kids, and I always think, "I ain't going to do that." Phil let his actions speak louder than his words. I think one of the most powerful things that happened to us as kids was when my oldest brother, Alan, was seventeen. He and his buddies went camping and were drinking beer. Then they decided to knock down a bunch of mailboxes up the road in a drunken redneck night. A neighbor came down the next morning and talked to Phil. Jase and I were pretty young, and we could hear the adults whispering in the kitchen. I remember hearing Phil say, "Okay, I got you." Phil walked out the front door, climbed in his truck, and drove off.

Phil drove to Alan's camp and found beer cans all over the ground. He told Alan to get in his truck. Then he told the three other boys, "If you ever want to come to my house for the rest of your life, get in my truck, and you're getting a whippin' for tearing up those mailboxes." Two of Alan's friends came over to our house pretty regularly, so they figured they'd better get in the truck. The third guy had never even seen Phil, and Al and the other two boys told him they wouldn't hold it against him if he didn't come. I guess he figured, "How bad can it really be?" The four of them climbed in the back of the truck, and Phil drove them back to our house. Jase and I hid in the azalea bushes and watched Phil whip four seventeen-year-old men. One of them was Bill "Red Dawg" Phillips, who was one of Alan's best friends and later worked for Duck Commander and appeared in several Duckmen videos. Phil told him, "I've known you all your life. I'm so disappointed. I can't believe you pulled a stunt like this." Greg Eppinette, who would later become one of our cameramen on the Duckmen videos, was also there. Phil told him, "I know your parents. We've been to church together. You tell your daddy why you got this." Then Phil whipped him. Next was the boy Phil had never laid eyes on. "Son," Phil said, "I don't know who you are but you tell your daddy that I whipped you and why I did it, and if he has a problem with it, he can come talk to me." Last was Alan, who was wearing these short little running shorts. It was the 1980s, and he looked like Richard Simmons. You want to talk about influencing young ones. It hurt Jase and me to watch that belt hitting Alan's pasty thighs. That was pretty much all it took to keep Alan in line for the rest of high school, and Jase and me as well.

After raising four kids, I think discipline has to start when they're young. A lot of our friends will say, "Oh, he's out of control," and their son is ten years old. I'm always thinking, "He's probably going to be out of control when he's eighteen. You missed it." By the time a kid is ten years old, his parents have missed their window of opportunity to really lay down the ground rules. I'm not saying it's over, I'm just saying the sooner you start teaching your kids what is expected and being consistent with your discipline, the better. Kids respond better when the boundaries are clearly defined. All of our children are old enough now that spankings are pretty much a thing of the past. I know that they will continue to find ways

THE SOONER YOU START TEACHING YOUR KIDS WHAT IS EXPECTED AND BEING CONSISTENT WITH YOUR DISCIPLINE, THE BETTER.

to test our boundaries, but disrespect is not tolerated, and if I see even an ounce of it, I promise, I can still think of some ways to make them regret it.

Of course, John Luke and Sadie always tell Will and Bella that they have it a lot easier. But I think the two younger kids saw how the two older kids acted, and they learned that's what was expected of them. If the two older kids were terrors, then the two younger kids would have probably ended up being terrors, too.

Korie: Willie commands respect from our kids because they know there is always going to be an immediate reaction if they misbehave. You have to discipline out of love, and there are lots of ways you can do that. We discipline them because we love them and we want to help them to grow into happy, healthy adults. Now that John Luke and Sadie are teenagers, they say that we are more relaxed than their friends' parents. We don't have to do much discipline anymore because we instilled that respect when they were young. And I have to say, we have really good kids. Of course, our kids aren't perfect. We've been on trips where everything was great until the ride home. Will and Bella will start arguing over something ridiculous, and they turn into typical nine- and ten-year-old kids. They'll have their struggles and their difficult times, but they know that we love them and will always be there for them, no matter if they're "a policeman or a jail person." They're ours!

Sometimes people ask us if we're worried how the fame will affect our kids. You know what? We're all in the same boat. Everybody is trying to raise their kids to be compassionate, loving, and responsible adults. There are some famous people who have kids who have messed up, but there are people working at a mill whose kids have messed up. We're all doing the best we can to raise our children. It's not really about fame. It's about spending time with your children, disciplining them when they need it, praising them when they need it, and letting them know they're loved.

All right, enough about our awesome kids. I hope you don't think we are saying we are the perfect parents or have the perfect family. Far from it! We do try to glorify God in the way we treat one another and the way we raise our children, and then we ask God to do the rest. Many of you reading this could certainly teach us a thing or two about marriage and child rearing, but these are just some things that we've done in our home, and if they help any of you, then it was worth writing it.

I HATE TO ADMIT IT, BUT I'LL JUST GO AHEAD AND THROW IT OUT THERE: I'M NOT THE COOK THAT KAY IS. OKAY, I'M NOT EVEN HALF THE COOK KAY IS.

Korie: You may have been wondering why we named this chapter "Fast Food." Well, I hate to admit it, but I'll just go ahead and throw it out there: I'm not the cook that Kay is. Okay, I'm not even half the cook Kay is. That's why on *Duck Dynasty* you always see me chopping vegetables. It's a joke around here that in every scene I'm in with Kay, I'm always chopping veg-etables. Willie says I put my apron on to toss the salad. I'm just not a good cook. I'm always rushed and have a hundred other things going on, so I burn the bread, or I'll start cooking something and realize I don't have the main ingredient!

Willie's the cook in our house. He is incredible. He can just throw a bunch of stuff together along with something he caught or brought out of the woods and it turns into a gour-met meal. Am I ever thankful that I married a man who can cook! The problem is, when he is not around, I am helpless. The kids and I have to survive on breakfast for supper. I'm good at pancakes, bacon and eggs, or something easy like tacos, but that's about the extent of it.

I promise I tried. When we got married, Kay gave me all of her recipes, along with a set of my own black skil-lets. I cooked for a while, but the more kids I had, the worse I seemed to get. I just couldn't do it all, and I had to admit it just wasn't my thing. Willie says he retired me from the kitchen when Will and Bella came along. It doesn't bother me. I'm good at a lot of things. Cooking just doesn't happen to be one of them. I'm good at being a mom; Willie's good at cook-ing. It works for us.

So, having said all that, I have to tell you that sometimes—well, more often than I care to admit—we just eat fast food. There, I said it. The end of every episode of *Duck Dynasty* shows us all around the dinner table, and that's real. It's what we do. We love to get together and enjoy a big meal together as a family. We do it often, but not every day. Sometimes we just go through the drive-through line and talk about our day in the car on the way to the next sporting event, and then we wait for Daddy to get home from his latest hunting or business trip so he can whip us up one of his gourmet meals!

HOMEMADE MAC AND CHEESE

Korie: This is an easy mac and cheese recipe that both kids and adults love. It is one of Kay's recipes that I make often. It's so easy, I can even do it!

1 package (16 ounces) large elbow macaroni
8 tablespoons butter
salt and pepper to taste
8 tablespoons flour
2½ cups milk
2 cups cheddar cheese, grated

1. Cook macaroni according to package directions.
2. While macaroni is boiling, melt butter on medium heat in a medium-sized saucepan and add salt, pepper, and flour. Stir continuously.
3. When butter is melted, add milk.
4. Stir until it thickens, then turn off heat.
5. Strain the macaroni and pour it into a pan.
6. Cover with butter sauce and mix together.
7. Add grated cheese on the top and put in oven at 350 degrees until the cheese is melted.

FRIED BURGERS

WHAT, THEN, SHALL WE SAY IN RESPONSE TO THESE
THINGS? IF GOD IS FOR US, WHO CAN BE AGAINST US?
—ROMANS 8:31

If you've watched *Duck Dynasty,* you know all about Kay's skills in the kitchen, but don't overlook Phil when it comes to cooking. One of Phil's specialties has always been good ol' hamburgers. Of course, they're not ordinary burgers. There is a very specific way that Phil cooks a burger. Most people put a patty of meat on the grill and just mash the heck out of it with a spatula, squeezing all the juice out of it as they try to cook it as fast as possible. But Phil's philosophy is to never put a spatula on a burger. Phil's famous burgers are not cooked on a grill—although he does grill burgers, but that's a whole 'nother story. His famous burgers are cooked on a griddle or in a frying pan. They just taste better that way. While most people take about a quarter-pound of hamburger and make as big of a patty as they can, Phil prefers smaller, thinner patties. Phil never takes any shortcuts with his cooking, so he applies more pepper than needed, and the cooking surface is a lot hotter than required. When Phil throws a patty on the griddle, he sears one side and then the other, locking in all the juices that give a burger its flavor. He browns his buns on the griddle and they soak up the grease, which makes them taste even better. Phil's burgers are some of the best around.

When I got older and had my own place, I started cooking my version of Phil's burgers. I cook them kind of like Phil does, but I've changed some things to make them my own. Phil taught me a long time ago that there's no use in changing something if it works, so I still cook my burgers on a griddle or in a pan, use thin patties, and toast my buns in grease, just like he does. But to make them different, I've at times added jalapeños, bacon, onions, different seasonings, and even blue cheese to the meat. I've covered them with all kinds of different cheeses. We started calling my burgers "Willie burgers." You know your burger is good when people start calling it by name. "Willie burgers" have become kind of famous among our family and friends, and there's a big debate as to whether my burgers or Phil's taste better.

Cooking burgers is pretty easy, which is probably why they're so popular at barbecues or when you're sitting by the swimming pool on the weekends. Not everyone can cook them well, but anyone can cook them. You fire up a grill or griddle and go to work. I feel like it's kind of that way in business, too. From day one, Duck Commander wasn't anything flashy. It started with a pretty common man with a very big dream. With the exception of Phil's invention of the double-reed duck call, the things we've done with Duck Commander over the years haven't necessarily been revolutionary. We didn't bring in a consultant from Harvard Business School to create a business model or strategic plan for us. In fact, very little of what we've done has been by the book, but I think we took some chances and risks over the years in our quest to make Duck Commander a success. Some of them worked out; some of them didn't.

I like to joke that the Robertson family and bad ideas go together like biscuits and jam. Every action in life begins with a decision, and unfortunately, we don't always make the best ones. Indeed, we've made some bad decisions over the years, but we wouldn't be where we are today without having taken some risks. Even when we faced tough times and what seemed like insurmountable odds, we persevered through our mistakes and landed on our feet again. We've always thought that if we did what was morally and ethically right, while continuing to steadfastly believe in what we were doing, we'd be okay in the end. More than anything else, Duck Commander is about building solid products, fostering relationships that last, and treating our employees like family. Well, most of us are family!

> I LIKE TO JOKE THAT THE ROBERTSON FAMILY AND BAD IDEAS GO TOGETHER LIKE BISCUITS AND JAM.

Even after Korie and I took over Duck Commander in 2005, Phil was still the king. I didn't immediately start making rogue decisions when I became CEO, and I wasn't interested in changing the way we'd done business for the previous thirty-something years. I never thought, "I'm going to change this, and I don't care what Phil thinks." I always went to him for advice before making a big decision, and he still has a very influential voice in how we operate today. There's a reason Duck Commander was already a solid business when I took it over, and it started with the foundation Phil built in the early days. We follow pretty simple business practices and we've stuck to them, even in turbulent times. Phil was determined to build his company with his family, and that's something that's really important to me as well. Unlike a lot of modern businessmen, Phil wasn't going to let his career get in the way of his family. That's an attribute pretty much anybody can respect and appreciate.

Korie: Phil and Willie are so much alike. We went to a marriage seminar at our church one time, and Phil and Kay and Jase and Missy were there as well. Each of the couples took a personality test to see if their personalities were compatible. We all laughed because Phil and Willie scored high in the characteristics for having a dominant personality. They were almost identical in a lot of areas, but somewhat different in that Willie was high in the social category as well. I think Willie got that part of his personality from his mother.

It's funny because people look at the Robertsons and think Jase and Phil are just alike, and they are certainly similar in their love for ducks. But when we took the personality test, we saw that Jase's personality is much more like his mother's. So I guess it makes sense that Phil and Jase get along so well in the duck blind. They make a good team, just like Phil and

Kay do at home. Kay has always said that Willie is a lot like Phil and even calls him "Phil Jr." at times. While I wouldn't go that far, I definitely see the similarities. They both have strong, charismatic personalities. They are both big-picture guys with big ideas and deep beliefs. Whatever either of them is doing in life, he does it all the way, and they are both very opinionated, which can sometimes be a challenge. Phil and Willie haven't always been as close as they are now. As they grew, they recognized the attributes they have in common and learned to value one another's differences and strengths. Willie says it couldn't have happened until after he was thirty, though. He needed to grow up and mature, and Phil has gotten more relaxed as he's gotten older. Willie loves to hunt with his dad and brothers, but there have been times when he's had a hard time sitting in Phil's blind. You can only have one leader in the duck blind, only one man who lines up the men and yells, "Cut 'em!" when it's time to shoot. Willie and Phil have both always been leaders, whether it's in the blind or in business.

YOU CAN ONLY HAVE ONE LEADER IN THE DUCK BLIND.

After I took over Duck Commander from Phil, not all of my decisions were popular. When we started *Benelli Presents Duck Commander* on the Outdoor Channel in 2009, while it was hugely successful and helped change hunting shows for the better, it was quite different for people who grew up watching our Duckmen videos. They were used to seeing Phil biting ducks' heads and watching ducks fall from the sky in slow motion. Really, our hard-core fans were used to seeing us kill a lot of ducks. But the show on Outdoor Channel revealed a lot of the business side of Duck Commander as well, which gave viewers a behind-the-scenes look at the company and our operations. Some people really liked seeing those aspects of Duck Commander, but change is hard for some people and there were some hard-core fans who only wanted to see the Duckmen shooting ducks from a blind for an hour. I can certainly appreciate both sides of the argument.

Korie: We started catching a little bit of flak from some of our longtime fans, and a lot of their criticism was aimed at Willie because he'd recently taken over the company. On the forums on our website, some people told us they liked the way the old videos were filmed and accused Willie of trying to ruin the company. They said Duck Commander was getting too corporate and too big, and it was all Willie's fault. After a while, I'd had enough. I couldn't stand it any longer. People didn't realize that Willie was trying to make Duck Commander financially solvent, and with the TV show, he was appealing to a much broader audience. In the old days, Phil made just enough money to pay the bills and feed his family.

But as Jase, Willie, and Jep got older and started working for the company, there were a lot more families to feed. Each of the Robertson boys had his own wife and children to provide for. There are a lot of other Duck Commander employees to pay as well, and most of them are our relatives and very close friends. Willie had to find ways to increase Duck Commander's revenue, or we were going to have to start laying people off, which we certainly didn't want to do. Putting a Duck Commander hunting show on the Outdoor Channel was one of the best decisions we made. We got new sponsors who were paying us money to wear and use their products, and, of course, there were contractual obligations that came with those agreements.

After I'd read enough of the complaints, I wrote a blog entry on our website entitled "Stand by Your Man." I explained to the disgruntled fans that Willie was only trying to make Duck Commander better, and that without the changes he made they wouldn't be able to see Phil, Jase, and Si shooting ducks anywhere, because there wouldn't be enough money to produce the DVDs. Willie wasn't out to change the core of what Duck Commander was. After all, he's Phil's son, so it's his heritage as well. He was just trying to expand the company and grow it into something even more people could appreciate and love. To this day, we still make the hunting DVDs for the serious duck hunters just like we did in the old days. I think people slowly started to realize that Duck Commander was really a business and it had bills to pay and expenses like any other company. And after my diatribe, the fans who were complaining on our forums apologized for criticizing Willie and we all made up!

Believe it or not, Phil has been making the hunting DVDs for more than two decades. The first ones were actually filmed on VHS tapes. Phil was convinced there was a market for waterfowl hunting videos when perhaps no one else was. There were a lot of deer- and other big-game-hunting videos on the market at the time, but no one had really tried it with ducks. Phil rented camera equipment from a company in Dallas and hired Gary Stephenson, a science teacher at Ouachita Christian School, to direct and film his first video. Much like Phil's duck calls, not a lot of other people believed the videos would be a success. *Duckmen 1: Duckmen of Louisiana* was released in 1988 and sold about one hundred copies. Undeterred, Phil set out to film *Duckmen 2: Point Blank,* which took the next five seasons to produce. Obviously, it was a very laborious venture and none of the Duckmen knew much of anything about filmmaking.

Like almost everything else Phil put his hands on, the Duckmen hunting tapes were unlike what everyone else was doing at the time. The videos lasted about an hour each and were among the first to include rock music over hunting scenes. Phil has always been a big fan of classic rock. He loves

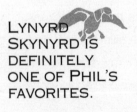

LYNYRD SKYNYRD IS DEFINITELY ONE OF PHIL'S FAVORITES.

Lynyrd Skynyrd, Led Zeppelin, Creedence Clearwater Revival, Pink Floyd, and Bob Seger. I still remember when Pink Floyd's *The Wall* came out in 1979. Phil bought the eight-track and plugged it in Alan's player, and then he just lay in the bed and listened to the entire tape. Lynyrd Skynyrd is definitely one of his favorites, though.

If there's one rule at Phil's house, it's that you never wake him while he's napping. It was a rule when I was a kid, and it's still that way today. One day, one of the members of Lynyrd Skynyrd called the Duck Commander office, which at that time was Phil and Kay's house, wanting to talk to Phil. I can't remember who answered the phone at the time, but he or she wasn't about to wake up Phil from his nap. Phil was so mad when he found out. He told us, "From this day forward, wake me up if the president of the United States or Lynyrd Skynyrd calls!"

I grew up listening to classic rock but then started liking country music when I was in college. Phil couldn't understand why I liked listening to it. While I was home from college for a break one time, a bunch of Phil's buddies were over at his house, and Phil called me down and started making fun of me for listening to country music. He told me rock 'n' roll was the only music worth listening to. I got mad, stormed out of the house, and said I was never coming back. I told you we were both opinionated! Of course, Phil listens to country music now.

Rock music wasn't the only thing different about the Duckmen videos. Phil, Jase, Si, and I have the long beards, and so did most of the other original Duckmen, Mac Owen, Dane Jennings, and Bill "Red Dawg" Phillips. Phillips was the first Duckman to paint his face. "Red Dawg" couldn't grow a long beard. His beard was pitiful, so he figured he'd paint his face to look different than the rest of us. After a while, Phil figured out paint was the best way to camouflage our white faces from the ducks. After all, a man's face stands out like a white surrender flag in a duck blind. Before too long, everyone in Phil's blind was required to wear face paint. By the time *Duckmen 3: In Yo' Face* came out in 1997, the videos had a pretty large cult following. There were a lot of funny and uncouth antics involved, like spitting contests, shooting water moccasins (a.k.a. congos or ol' Jims, as Phil likes to call them), and picking the feathers off ducks. The hunting scenes were really kind of in your face and over the top. In *Duckmen 2*, Phil flipped a deer with a rifle shot, which the cameraman, Greg Eppinette, captured in slow motion. Phil became nearly as famous for flipping the deer as any of his duck hunting. There was definitely a shock value to the early Duckmen videos. We released our sixteenth Duckmen video in 2012, and they're still very popular.

As we began to grow and develop more relationships in the hunting industry, many people started telling us we should get our own TV show, but we really couldn't figure out how it was going to make money. I did not know anything about the business side of hunting shows. I knew I had to learn everything I could about this venture before I jumped into it. I felt I had a good grasp on entertainment but needed to know the financial side, because one thing we didn't have at that time was a lot of money. Duck Commander was still operating on a very tight budget.

Most hunting shows are paid programming, so you have to buy the airtime from a network and sell the advertisements on your own. And most hunting shows don't make money, but companies write it off as advertising. I didn't feel like I had the money to invest in something like that at the time. But we knew we would have a really good product if we could ever do it, because Duck Commander had so many unique personalities.

About this same time reality shows were really taking off. Korie liked watching reality TV, and we became convinced our family had what it took to venture into it. After seeing *American Chopper,* we were even more convinced our family could have its own show. People weren't watching *American Chopper* because they loved motorcycles. The success of that show was due to the big personalities and the relationships between the dad and his sons. We knew we had that and then some!

We caught a break when Steve Kramer, an in-house producer with Benelli Shotguns, went on a hunting trip to Arkansas with Phil, Jase, Jep, and me. Kramer watched how we interacted and listened to our stories about our antics in the duck blind. He had a background in reality TV and was producing commercials for Benelli. When we went to SHOT Show a couple of months later, Kramer called us into a meeting. He told us Benelli thought we could do a TV show and went over what he thought the show could be. It was exactly what Korie and I had been talking about! We just kept looking across the table at one another with smiles on our faces. We were very much on the same page with what Kramer was laying out creatively. But then we told him we couldn't afford to produce a show. He said he thought Benelli would be willing to back it financially, although they would need me to help get other sponsors on board as well. Benelli would be willing to put its name on the show for advertising, even if it could not recoup the money it was going to invest. It didn't happen right away, however. When we left the meeting, I said, "Let me try to talk Phil into doing it." Kramer said, "We've got to work out the details with Steve McKelvain [Benelli's vice president of marketing]." Almost a full year went by before cameras rolled.

Kramer was our executive producer, and the show swept the Golden Moose Awards the first year, which are kind of like the Oscars for outdoor TV. Kramer brought a lot to the table, and the quality was different from anything else on outdoor TV. He was passionate about making the show the best it could be creatively and stylistically. Benelli produced the first two seasons of *Duck Commander* but then decided it couldn't pay for the production costs anymore. It was a really expensive show to produce by hunting-show standards. By that time, though, we were able to take it on ourselves. We hired Warm Springs Productions, which had worked with us in season one, to produce season three.

Phil was really never convinced that the show on Outdoor Channel would work. "Who's gonna watch this?" he proclaimed. But I told Phil he had to trust me on the idea and that the move would help our business. He reluctantly agreed to do it, and from day one I worked very hard to make sure it would not be miserable for him. His reluctance gave me the motivation to make sure it was successful. Duck Commander's sales grew, and the show gave the entire company a new spirit—a spirit

> I TOLD PHIL HE HAD TO TRUST ME ON THE IDEA AND THAT THE MOVE WOULD HELP OUR BUSINESS. HE RELUCTANTLY AGREED.

of confidence. It was cool seeing the fans' reactions to the episodes at hunting shows, signing autographs, and selling more products. But more than anything else, it was preparing us for something so much bigger.

Now, the Lord works in mysterious ways for sure. In September 2010, we found an e-mail in one of the generic boxes at DuckCommander.com. It was from Scott Gurney, who owned Gurney Productions, a TV production company in Los Angeles. Gurney wrote that he knew of *Duck Commander,* watched our show on Outdoor Channel, and really thought we had what it takes to go to the next level. One of our employees called me and asked if he should call Gurney back. He forwarded me the e-mail and I took it from there. I called Scott and we talked for a few hours. He was a big thinker and got me really excited about what he thought we could do. At one point, Scott said, "Man, you get a show on a major network, you will sell T-shirts in Walmart."

"We already sell T-shirts in Walmart," I told him.

"Oh, yeah, I keep forgetting you guys have a big following," Gurney told me.

As we're about to start our second season of *Duck Dynasty* on A&E, I get asked this question all the time: "How did you end up getting a show on a major network? How did they find you?" Everyone wants to know how you end up doing a reality TV show. Well, that's how we did it. Most folks don't do a show on a small network and then get discovered. But looking back, the experience we had on Outdoor Channel was invaluable. That's where we learned our craft of making great TV. It was where we got a taste for fame, became prepared, and learned to focus. We witnessed the ins and outs of making television shows, and learned how to work on TV schedules, and, perhaps most important, saw what worked and what didn't. Oh, did we learn!

We didn't know A&E would be where we would end up. We made a highlights video, or "sizzle reel," as it's called in Hollywood, and Gurney pitched it to the networks. It was well received by many of them, but Gurney called and said A&E was most interested. Our only experience with A&E up to this point had been an appearance on an episode of *Billy the Exterminator* the year before, when Billy and Ricky came to West Monroe to exterminate our duck blinds. As far as I know, that was the only time Billy and Ricky had to literally abort the mission! Our blind was full of snakes and, even worse for Ricky, wasps. Unfortunately, Ricky is allergic to wasps and got stung right on his nose. The producers called "Cut!" and rushed Ricky to the hospital! That was the end of our filming with A&E up to this point.

Gurney told us that A&E wanted to do two episodes and if they liked them, they would pick up a full season. It wasn't a guarantee. Initially, we had bigger offers from some other networks, but let's face it, this was A&E we were talking about! And Gurney said that it was where we needed to be. We were still cautious, though. If A&E didn't like the episodes, nothing would happen, so we didn't tell too many people about the opportunity at first. We just kind of quietly made the episodes and waited to see what happened.

Thankfully, A&E's executives liked what they saw. The show turned out funnier than even we expected. When we watched it for the first time as a family, we laughed the entire way through. Phil even said, "Willie, you might be right. I think this could work."

I basically bet the farm that having a TV show would do wonders for our company, and it did. When the *Duck Commander* show came out on Outdoor Channel, our sales numbers began to increase. Then when *Duck Dynasty* began airing on A&E, the growth was absolutely phenomenal. I really cannot even explain what the growth has been like. The crew at our warehouse is work-

> I BASICALLY BET THE FARM THAT HAVING A TV SHOW WOULD DO WONDERS FOR OUR COMPANY.

ing their tails off to keep up. I'm so proud of the growth that we made while still staying true to our roots. I am proud to say that I proved Phil wrong on the whole TV venture. A&E is absolutely a first-class network. They have been so cool to work with. Phil had big reservations about doing the show, but I persuaded him on the idea. A&E wanted to do a dinner scene with a prayer at the end of every episode. I told Phil that it would be a chance for us to show America a family that loves each other and was, dare I say, positive in so many ways. This wasn't only a sales pitch to Phil because I really believed God had called us for something truly special.

And I guess the rest is history, 'cause we're still sharing our message on TV. *Duck Dynasty* is kind of like Phil's burgers. He took something very simple and made it into something that people have talked about for years. Phil made VHS tapes of his duck hunts, and I tried to make them better. I still remember when I told Phil we should switch from VHS tapes to DVDs and he thought I was crazy. Phil laid the groundwork with the Duckmen videos, and I just added to them. I make the same type of burger Phil does, but just added a little to them and make them for a future generation. The idea behind the burger is the same as Dad's, just with some glitz and glamour. And by the way, when I'm at Phil's house and he's making burgers, I'm the first in line to eat about three of them. They are fabulous.

WILLIE BURGERS

I usually just make my burgers plain, just meat and salt and black pepper, especially for the family. Blue Cheese is my favorite add-on if you want to take them up a notch. I can knock out eight to ten burgers in fifteen minutes. My kids' favorite side is my fries: I peel potatoes, cut them up in slivers, fry them in peanut oil, and immediately apply Cajun seasoning, and then I throw a pinch of sugar on (shhhhh, that's my secret). Do all this while they are still piping hot—you wait, you lose.

1 pound ground round
salt and pepper to taste
Phil Robertson's Cajun Style Seasoning, to taste
8 ounces blue cheese
1 package bacon
hamburger buns

1. Make hamburger patties that are small and thin, mixing in the blue cheese if you wish.
2. Generously season hamburger patties with salt, pepper, and Cajun Style Seasoning.
3. Cook bacon.
4. Sear one side of hamburger for about 3 to 4 minutes, but never touch it with a spatula (and don't push out the juices!). Then flip the hamburger once and don't touch it again.
5. Top with bacon.
6. Warm hamburger buns in the grease from the patties.

14

DUMPLINGS, HOT WATER, CORNBREAD, AND FRIED SQUIRRELS

A WIFE OF NOBLE CHARACTER WHO CAN FIND? SHE IS WORTH FAR
MORE THAN RUBIES. HER HUSBAND HAS FULL CONFIDENCE IN HER
AND LACKS NOTHING OF VALUE . . . HER CHILDREN ARISE AND
CALL HER BLESSED; HER HUSBAND ALSO, AND HE PRAISES HER.
—PROVERBS 31:10–11, 28

Before Korie and I started running Duck Commander, everything happened at Phil and Kay's house. That's where all of the duck-call manufacturing, packaging, shipping, and billing took place. Every Duck Commander employee worked at Phil and Kay's house, which is a pretty good ways out of town and not the ideal working situation. They are too far out of town to get regular cable or Internet service, so everything was on satellite. Every time it rained hard we would lose service. We'd be waiting on a big order and the lights would go out. Plus, the "offices" were only old buildings and old trailers that were pieced together as the company grew. About six years ago, Korie and I moved to a new house and relocated most of Duck Commander's business operations to our old house. We ran the website and did all of the clerical work there. The manufacturing was still taking place at Phil's house because that's where the machinery was located. But in the winter of 2008, the Ouachita River flooded its banks, and the water slowly made its way up to my parents' house.

I can still remember asking Phil how he was going to ship orders if his property flooded.

"Well, I guess we'll put them on a boat," Phil told me, with a scary sense of seriousness in his voice.

It was right in the middle of duck-hunting season, and Duck Commander was very busy. We couldn't afford to take a chance on my parents' house flooding, along with all of the duck calls that were being made down there. If there were any delays in our manufacturing or shipping, it would cost us a lot of money. So Korie and I purchased a warehouse from her father, Johnny. Duck Commander's employees were excited about working at the new warehouse because most of them lived in town and their drive wasn't going to be nearly as far. But they were also a little sad about leaving my parents' house because Kay had been cooking them lunch every workday for nearly four decades.

When Duck Commander was working out of Phil and Kay's

house, it was a very casual work atmosphere. Kay would cook a big meal for lunch every day, and they would all eat and then most of the employees would take a nap. Then they'd all sit around and talk. Eventually, they would get back to working. But if somebody got a hankering to go fishing, everybody just went fishing. I think moving to our old house was a good transition before moving it all to a warehouse in town. If we had gone straight to a big warehouse, everyone would have had a hard time adjusting. We've always strived to keep that family atmosphere that Kay and Phil started, while finding ways to become more efficient and productive. I think we've achieved that. If you ask around

> IF SOMEBODY GOT A HANKERING TO GO FISHING, EVERYBODY JUST WENT FISHING.

our offices, people will tell you that they actually like coming to work. It's a fun environment with people who love each other, have interesting personalities, and enjoy what they do. It doesn't get any better than that.

Kay was a little relieved to get everybody out of her kitchen and out of her house, but I think she felt a little sadness, too. She and Phil were so used to having so many people around the house all the time. They were kind of like, "Wait a minute. What are we going to do now?" Now Kay brings her grandkids down to the house and plans outings and fun things for them. And, of course, if Phil or Jase runs the nets and catches a big mess of catfish, all work stops at the warehouse while everyone heads down to Phil and Kay's for an impromptu fish fry. Kay still enjoys cooking for anyone who drops by, and the whole family joins in for dinner often. Kay's not getting off that easy!

At everyone's birthdays, Kay will cook the birthday girl or boy her or his favorite meal. Some of the meals that people always want Kay to cook are the ones she made when I was younger, like hot-water cornbread, dumplings, and fried squirrels. Those are still some of my favorites, too, and they always take me back to my childhood when I eat them. When I was little, we didn't have much money to buy groceries, so Kay made meals that were inexpensive and didn't require a lot of ingredients. She could make a meal for Phil and her four growing boys with about five bucks' worth of food, and there would usually be seconds for all of us.

Kay makes hot-water cornbread with cornmeal, salt, sugar, boiling water, and oil. Her cornbread is an old-fashioned recipe; she fries the cornbread cakes, rather than baking them, and they're delicious. Kay's dumplings involve simple ingredients as well (all-purpose flour, baking soda, baking powder, Crisco, and buttermilk), and the only things she needs to make fried squirrels are flour, seasoning, and oil. Of course, the squirrels are free and you can eat as many as you can shoot. You know what Kay says about squirrel brains—they make you smart! I guess Jase never ate enough of them when we were younger.

As you might guess, Kay takes quite a bit of pride in her cooking, and everyone brags about her food. But the Robertson men are not easy on her when she messes a meal up. Phil says the best way to ensure someone will continue to be a bad cook is to brag on bad cooking. That will never happen in the Robertson house.

PHIL SAYS THE BEST WAY TO ENSURE SOMEONE WILL CONTINUE TO BE A BAD COOK IS TO BRAG ON BAD COOKING.

A Robertson family tradition is eating seafood for Christmas dinner, and it's usually better than you could get at any five-star restaurant. But at our Christmas dinner in 1998, Kay fried the shrimp for way too long. Kay and Phil's shrimp are usually fried lightly, but not these; they were dark brown and tasted like rubber.

"Whoa, Kay, what happened, did you forget how to cook?" I asked her.

Phil was even more critical, but it was all in good fun.

"Don't you know you're only supposed to cook shrimp for three minutes?" Phil asked her. "These are terrible. I wouldn't even put them in my crawfish nets."

At every Christmas dinner since, we always ask Kay if she's going to serve overcooked shrimp and everyone has a good laugh at Kay's expense. She doesn't mind; she can dish it up as good as she can take it.

Korie: I ate those shrimp and thought they were delicious. But in the Robertson family you can't get away with anything. I think I burned the bread like once and Willie loves to joke that you know when dinner's ready at our house when you hear me scraping the bread! They're a tough crowd in the kitchen, but it's all in good fun. I tell people you have to have healthy self-esteem to be married to a Robertson.

Kay lived in a house full of Robertson boys and men, and I'm still not sure how she survived. There were Phil, me, and my three brothers, and there were usually a couple of our friends hanging around. But Kay has a lot of patience and has always been very funny—I think that's where I get my sense of humor—and she has a mechanism for turning anything into fun. I'm not sure Phil has ever really understood her humor. Jase and Phil are a lot more serious and have a much more dry sense of humor, so Kay and I are always making fun of them and have our inside jokes about them. Sometimes, Kay and I will be in the kitchen laughing together, and Phil will walk in and tell us we're being too noisy. He'll be trying to watch the late news and will say, "Hey, *Saturday Night Live* is over." Every time Phil walks out of the room, I'll make a face at him, almost behind his back. Phil says he doesn't even know how to laugh, while Kay is always jovial and constantly has a big smile on her face. You know what they say about how opposites attract.

Korie: The thing that has impressed me most about Kay is that she really rarely gets truly aggravated or mad at Phil and the boys. She knows how to not sweat the small stuff. She's been through a lot in her and Phil's marriage, and I think it taught her that most things are really not worth getting mad at. She has a really fun side to her. Willie and Jep are always putting food down her back, grabbing her from behind, or throwing something into her hair, and I'm sure it got pretty old about twenty years ago. At some point, most people would be like, "Okay, enough already." But Kay laughs every time. She doesn't take herself very seriously, which I think is one of the most important qualities for enjoying life and one I have made sure to try to pass on to our children.

One of the reasons Kay laughs so much now is because in the beginning, when Phil was drinking and they didn't have much money, there wasn't a lot of laughing going on. But now we laugh at almost everything together. On our birthdays, Kay likes to send us very random cards, like Earth Day or graduation cards. Her favorite thing to do at Christmas is to give us gag gifts. After we've exchanged gifts as a family, she'll give everybody a joke gift. Kay will often forget why she thought it was funny when she bought it. She'll give someone salt and pepper shakers and won't even remember why she gave them!

Of course, Kay's gifts always say they're from her dogs. If you get a present from her rat terriers—or some random famous person whose name is on the tag—you know it's actually one of Kay's gag gifts. Every one of Kay's rat terriers has been named Jesse James or some version of his name, because if one dies she'll still have another one with her. Somehow, that helps her cope with the trauma of losing one of her pets. She's had like twenty of those dogs and they've all been named Jesse, JJ, or Jesse James II. She calls one of her dogs Bo-Bo, but his real name is Jesse James.

Kay loves her dogs. One time, Phil chopped a copper-

> EVERY ONE OF KAY'S RAT TERRIERS HAS BEEN NAMED JESSE JAMES OR SOME VERSION OF HIS NAME.

head in three pieces with a shovel, and then he picked up the snake's head and threw it close to one of Kay's dogs. Even though the snake was cut in three pieces, it somehow managed to bite the dog's head and latch on to its eye. The dog's head swelled up like a basketball. Phil looked at me and said, "Don't tell your mother." I was like, "Uh-huh, she'll never notice." The dog was fine. These are country dogs; they can take a little snake venom and keep on going. Phil is always throwing dead snakes at dogs to see their reaction, but not the poisonous ones anymore. He's not going to take a chance on hurting one of Miss Kay's beloved dogs.

With Kay, everything is an exaggeration and every conversation with her centers around food. When I call their house to talk to Phil, if Kay answers the phone, I have to listen to what they ate for lunch that day or dinner the previous night. I might be calling to talk to Phil about a big business deal, but Kay only wants to talk about how she cooked green beans, ham, and fresh corn, or how she'd already cooked lunch, but then a couple more people came over so she pulled a couple packages of sausage out of the freezer. Then she'll ask you what you had for lunch and dinner, and she'll want to know exactly how you cooked it. She always wants to know the details. Every conversation with her involves food, and it's either the best thing she ever put in her mouth or it was a disaster. I'll never forget the time she cooked meatloaf for Phil and ran out of ketchup. She never runs out of ketchup and couldn't believe she'd let it happen. It was like the Japanese bombed Pearl Harbor again.

Korie: Kay is the most patient person I know. Phil, on the other hand, let's just say patience is not his virtue. When we were filming Kay's cooking video, *The Commander's Kitchen,* Phil was getting a little aggravated with me because he didn't want to wait to cook his frog legs. It was taking us a little while to set up the cameras and everything, and A&E was there to film an episode of *Duck Dynasty* so it took a lot longer than we expected. I kept telling Phil he had to wait to cook his frog legs until his scene. We were making a TV show, you know? But Phil didn't want to ruin his frog legs, so I kept catching him trying to cook them, and I kept telling him he had to wait, and he was getting more and more frustrated.

We finally got to the scene where Phil was supposed to cook the frog legs, but then the A&E producers interrupted him. Phil gave me a look that indicated he was finished. Making sure his frog legs were per-fect was the most important thing to him, not whether our cooking video or *Duck Dynasty* episode turned out right. I could only laugh and let him finish. Nobody tells Phil what to do, and I cer-tainly wasn't about to start. We made it work: he cooked the frog legs, and they tasted fantastic. This became the first episode of *Duck Dynasty* and we got a great cooking DVD out of it. It turned out to be a very good day.

> NOBODY TELLS PHIL WHAT TO DO, AND I CERTAINLY WASN'T ABOUT TO START.

I'm not sure Kay ever gets enough credit for helping our family and Duck Commander survive when times were tough.

Let's face it: if Kay hadn't been strong enough to forgive Phil for the way he acted when I was young, our family and consequently Duck Commander wouldn't be here today. Thankfully, Kay's heart was big enough to look past Phil's transgressions and remember the man she married. After Phil kicked us out of the house, Kay made a thorough examination of her life and surrendered herself to Jesus Christ. She knew forgiving Phil was the right thing to do for her sons. If she wouldn't have forgiven Phil for things he'd done, or if he hadn't made changes in his life, we wouldn't be here today. As Phil began his Christian walk, he realized Kay was the best thing that ever happened to him, and they've been happily married ever since.

During the past four decades, Phil and Kay have been through some very difficult times and tackled them together. In the early days of Duck Commander, Kay was burdened with how the bills were going to be paid. We sometimes joke about Kay's not finishing high school—she gets mad at me when I tease her about it because she did receive her GED after Alan was born—but I think it's pretty remarkable that she kept Duck Commander afloat for so long without having any kind of business background. When Phil started making duck calls, he was an excellent salesman, but other than that, he wanted nothing to do with the business side of the company. He just wanted to make his calls and hunt and fish.

Before Kay and Phil turned Duck Commander over to Korie and me, the company was doing over $1 million in sales. Kay was in charge of inventory, accounting, payroll, and bookkeeping, with the help of other members of the family, but she was the one primarily in charge, and she had absolutely zero business training. She'd worked for Howard Brothers Discount Stores for a while, but Kay was in no way trained to oversee a multimillion-dollar business. She didn't even have a desk! Every night, Phil would sit in a recliner in the living room, and Kay would sit by him at the end of the couch. She kept all of Duck Commander's bills and sales orders in a little basket and that's how she would run the business. It's incredible when you think about it; we never would have made it without her.

Korie: Willie has always wanted to impress Kay and help her as much as possible. He realized a long time ago that his mother was working extremely hard but never got much of the glory because Phil was the star of Duck Commander. Kay's role was absolutely critical in the early days of Duck Commander. When we were dating, Willie and I painted Kay's kitchen cabinets for her for Mother's Day. She had a little tiny kitchen back then with not even a dishwasher, yet she cooked for the family and all the Duck Commander employees every day. There was so much grease on those cabinets from years of cooking, it was a miracle we ever got it all off to paint over it. Willie's love for his parents has always motivated him to do special things for them and to take Duck Commander to the next level, and they have always been very supportive and appreciative of him. Whether Willie paints Kay's kitchen, builds her something in the yard, cooks a great meal, or lands a big business deal, Kay has a special knack for bragging on him that makes him feel like a million bucks. She actually does that for all of us, and especially her boys. Sometimes people think that you should motivate your kids or employees by yelling at them when they fail or pointing out all the things they did wrong, but just the opposite is true. God created us to thrive on encouragement from others. Kay figured that out a long time ago. She has the gift of encouragement and gives that gift to those she loves the most.

Whether it was in business or raising her family, Kay always managed to make it work even when times were hard and money was tight. Even though we have enough money now to eat big steaks, shrimp, and even lobster from time to time, we still love Kay's old-fashioned meals, like hot-water cornbread, dumplings, and fried squirrels. In a lot of ways, her home-cooked meals brought us comfort when we needed it most, and now they remind us of where we came from and how hard we worked to get where we are today, which none of us ever want to forget.

KAY HAS A SPECIAL KNACK FOR BRAGGING ON HIM THAT MAKES WILLIE FEEL LIKE A MILLION BUCKS.

HOT-WATER CORNBREAD

This is Southern cooking at its best, and nobody does it better than Miss Kay!

2½ cups yellow cornmeal (not self-rising)
1 teaspoon salt
1 tablespoon sugar
4 cups water, boiling
6 cups peanut oil

1. Mix cornmeal, salt, and sugar together.
2. Pour in boiling water, just until wet but not runny, stirring as you pour.
3. Heat oil in skillet.
4. Put your hands in ice water, because the mixture will be hot, then scoop out a small handful, pat out into a patty, then drop in skillet of hot oil. Fry until brown on both sides, then take out and put on paper towel. That's it! They're delicious!

FRIED SQUIRREL

1 small, young squirrel
salt and pepper to taste
2 cups all-purpose flour
peanut oil, for frying

1. Skin the squirrel and cut into 7 pieces: 4 legs, back, rib cage, and head.
2. Season with salt and pepper, then roll in flour.
3. Fry in hot peanut oil until brown.

BOILED SQUIRREL

This is the best way to cook older squirrel (big ones)!

1 large, older squirrel
salt and pepper to taste

One 12-ounce can evaporated milk
½ stick of butter

1. Skin the squirrel, then cut in half.
2. Boil squirrel in water seasoned generously with salt and pepper for about 15 minutes.
3. Touch with fork to make sure it is tender, then take out squirrel from broth and add evaporated milk and butter. Allow to simmer while making your dumplings.

DUMPLINGS

4 cups all-purpose flour
¾ teaspoon baking soda
5 teaspoons baking powder
1 teaspoon salt
3 tablespoons Crisco, Butter Flavor
2 cups buttermilk

1. Sift all dry ingredients.
2. Add Crisco and mix with a pastry blender.
3. Add buttermilk a little at a time, stirring the mixture until a soft ball forms (like the consistency of biscuit dough).
4. Lay out wax paper or a pastry sheet and sprinkle with flour.
5. Make dough into 4 balls and use a rolling pin to roll each ball out flat and thin If dough is too sticky add more flour. Cut into squares with a knife.
6. Bring squirrel broth to a boil. Make sure there is enough in the pot to fill at least half the pot. If there is not, add more water.
7. Drop dumplings into boiling broth a handful at a time. When they are all in, turn down heat to low, put lid on pot, and let simmer for 15 minutes.
8. Get out a bowl, add some dumplings and squirrel, and enjoy!

15

DUCK WRAPS

TWO ARE BETTER THAN ONE, BECAUSE THEY HAVE A GOOD RETURN
FOR THEIR LABOR: IF EITHER OF THEM FALLS DOWN, ONE CAN
HELP THE OTHER UP. BUT PITY ANYONE WHO FALLS AND HAS NO
ONE TO HELP THEM UP. ALSO, IF TWO LIE DOWN TOGETHER, THEY
WILL KEEP WARM. BUT HOW CAN ONE KEEP WARM ALONE? THOUGH
ONE MAY BE OVERPOWERED, TWO CAN DEFEND THEMSELVES.
A CORD OF THREE STRANDS IS NOT QUICKLY BROKEN.
—ECCLESIASTES 4:9–12

Someone once said to Korie that as the CEO of Duck Commander, I'm not accountable to anyone. But in reality, I'm accountable to everyone. If the company doesn't make it, then we're all out of work. And since most of our employees are also our relatives and friends, it's a heck of a lot of pressure to carry every day. I know the decisions I make affect everyone in my family, from Phil and Kay to Alan, Jase, and Jep and their families, as well as Korie and our children. Phil and Kay trust me to do the job because they know I recognize the burden and know I take the responsibility of running the family business very seriously.

It means a lot to me that my dad started this whole thing.

Phil launched Duck Commander and poured his heart and soul into it. It's his life's work. But I also think he would have never gotten the credit and recognition he deserved if we hadn't taken Duck Commander to another level. Changes had to be made, or Duck Commander would have suffered the same fate as a lot of other duck-call companies. Many of the guys who started out in the hunting industry when Phil launched Duck Commander in 1973 aren't around anymore. Several of them went through the same cycle: a father with a love for the outdoors starts a company, it has some success in the beginning, but if the next generation doesn't pick up the torch, and they just dwindle back down to where they first started, with a couple of guys making duck calls, or they fade away altogether. They still go to hunting shows, set up a little table, and sell their goods, but they haven't reached the success or had the longevity Duck Commander has. Now, there is certainly nothing wrong with setting up a table and selling your wares. In fact it reminds me of the old days for us. We were not big back then, but we had some good times at those hunting festivals.

When Korie and I took over the company, Phil told us that Duck Commander had begun to slide after its peak a few years earlier. Walmart sales were starting to go away and there was not a whole lot of traction in other stores, either. Buyers were starting to go to "full line" companies, which could sell them not only duck calls but also many other calls. It was harder and harder for companies who sold only one product to even get a sales meeting. Phil wasn't panicked or upset, he just felt that it was the life cycle of business and was proud of what he had accomplished up to that point. Duck Commander would have ended up being a very small business, probably only employing Phil, Kay, Jase, and Missy and maybe one other person, like it did in the early days. The ideas were getting fewer and fewer, the market was changing, Kay was stressed out, and Phil and Kay were just weary. I think Korie and I came at the right time and brought a lot of energy and excitement because we were young and had an entirely fresh look at it. Once the ball started rolling, other people became energized and the excitement was kind of contagious.

Every one of our employees at Duck Commander had an integral role in getting the company to where it is today. As I told you earlier, I'm a big baseball fan and Duck Commander is like a team. You have your flashier players, but you still need your utility men and middle relievers. You see people like Jase and Si on *Duck Dynasty* every week, but there are a lot of people doing really important jobs behind the scenes to make Duck Commander work.

When I took over, I was able to watch what was going on from afar and make some big changes, some that were popular and some that weren't. I had to fire some people and hired some people that others didn't think we needed. Everybody wanted to make more money than they were getting, and they thought they were probably going to get even less because we were bringing in additional people. One of the first hires I made that proved to be a really good one was Becky McDaniel, our accountant. After looking at Duck Commander's financial books, I realized Kay was spending about $35,000 a year on late fees, penalties, and finance charges. It wasn't Kay's fault; she was only trying to keep the company open when it was stretched to the max. Kay was doing the best she could and was simply overwhelmed. But in the end, hiring Becky was worth eliminating the monthly late fees and finance charges we'd been paying for so long. Becky has become an integral part of Duck Commander, doing much more than just accounting. She knows every part of the business and I can trust her to keep things rolling while Korie and I start new projects like making television shows.

Of course, it's never easy when you're related to most of your employees. You saw on the show what happened when I tried to put the guys through team-building exercises. They don't always listen to what I say or do what I want, but it's a lot more fun working with the people you care about the most. It also has its challenges. Like Uncle Si says, it's never a good family reunion when you start firing relatives.

My brother Jase is Phil's right-hand man in the blind and mine at Duck Commander. He went to seminary after high school, then worked for the church for a little while, but essentially came straight to work at Duck Commander. He loves ducks as much as Phil does and is the expert when it comes to duck calls. He takes what he does very seriously. He studies ducks and knows how to imitate their exact sounds. He doesn't settle for Duck Com-

> LIKE UNCLE SI SAYS, IT'S NEVER A GOOD FAMILY REUNION WHEN YOU START FIRING RELATIVES.

mander calls sounding okay. He wants them to be perfect. He'll spend the same amount of time tuning a call for a beginner duck caller who doesn't know what he's doing as he will for an expert caller who has been hunting for years. Making duck calls is one of his passions, and he just loves doing it. I think he especially likes the camaraderie of all the guys sitting around blowing a little smoke between blowing the duck calls. He doesn't like the stress of things changing and being different. Sitting in a chair and doing the same thing every day would drive me absolutely crazy, but I think that's part of what Jase likes about his work.

Korie: Jase lives right across the street from us, and he and his wife, Missy, have three kids: Reed, Cole, and Mia. Jase and Missy like to joke that our oldest son, John Luke, is like Kramer from *Seinfeld*. On nights when we're not cooking at our house, John Luke busts through their front door as soon as he sees the dining room light go on to join them for dinner. He seems to know exactly when Missy pulls the rolls out of the oven. Our baby girl, Bella, and their daughter, Mia, are great friends. We say Mia is like the ghost of our house. She appears in our house at all times. You'll turn around in your recliner, and she'll be standing there. As soon as we pull in the driveway, she's in our house, waiting to play with Bella. Our entire neighborhood is actually family. My parents are next door, along with four aunts and uncles and two grandparents. That's the absolute best thing about where we live. It's all about family.

I'm really proud of my youngest brother, Jep, who has grown up and become a good man. Jep was always like a little tree in a big forest. He was the youngest Robertson son, and his older brothers never lacked confidence. And of course, Phil was bigger than life, so Jep always kind of grew up in our shadows. Jep came along at a different time, too. When he was born, my mom and dad finally had a little bit of money. You know how poor people are when they get their hands on money. Everything had to be the nicest and the best for Jep, so he had a much different experience growing up than the rest of us. He didn't have to work like we did when we were younger, and I think a lot of things were handed to him. I think Jep probably needed more guidance and didn't get it. He ended up a little wayward and was kind of just hanging around.

When I took over Duck Commander, Jep was working at the company but wasn't really super ambitious and wasn't sure what he wanted to do with his life. Jep was my brother, so I was going to give him some breaks for sure, but I wasn't going to let him keep making the same mistakes and keep getting away with what he was doing. He was coming to work whenever he felt like it. I remember one time Jep was gone for like a month. Everybody thought that maybe he was out of town, but nobody knew for sure. I called Jep into my office when he finally came back to the warehouse. He was my brother, so I knew I couldn't fire him. But I couldn't allow Jep to keep making the same mistakes because it wasn't fair to our other employees and was bad for morale.

"Let me tell you something," I told him. "I ain't going to fire you. But what I am going to do is put a time clock in here. You're going to clock in and clock out every day. You're going to start out at your full salary. But if your time slip goes down, you're going to get less money. I'm not going to fire you, but if you're only making a thousand dollars per year, you're going to want to go work someplace else."

After a few months, Jep decided he wanted to go to work on the offshore oil rigs because he wanted to make more money. I thought it was maybe what Jep needed to do because he'd never worked anyplace other than Duck Commander. I thought maybe Jep needed to go find out what it was like to have a boss who wasn't part of his family.

"Hey, do what you've got to do, brother," I told him.

But the next day, I called Jep back into my office. "You've got to do what you've got to do," I told him again. "But let me tell you this: you're a stupid idiot if you leave this company. I'm fixin' to turn this thing around and you won't be here. You're going to miss out. Phil has four boys, and your last name is Robertson. There's an advantage you have in life just because you're Phil Robertson's son. You can take advantage of that working here, or you can go work in an oil field. They don't care what your last name is out there. You're going to lose every advantage you have in life and what Dad built for you. You're going to go trade it all for something like that?" I knew that if the dreams I had for our company came to fruition, I wanted Jep to be a part of it, and I couldn't just let him give it all up without saying something.

Fortunately, Jep didn't leave the company. We just had to find out what his talents were and take advantage of them. For a while, Jep decided that to make extra money he was going to start doing sales calls. I handed Jep a list of clients and told him to knock himself out. After two or three days, he came back into my office and said sales wasn't his cup of tea. But we found his gift. Jep has turned into an excellent cameraman. He shoots our Duckmen videos and does a lot of editing. Phil brags about how no one can capture ducks like Jep does. You have to be a hunter to do it, and Jep knows exactly how ducks fly and where he needs to be at all times to capture them on film. Plus, Jep isn't as outgoing as Jase and me, so he works well behind a camera. He loves to hunt but doesn't mind being a guy who sits and watches the action, and that's something Jase and I could never do.

WE JUST HAD TO FIND OUT WHAT HIS TALENTS WERE AND TAKE ADVANTAGE OF THEM.

Plus, I really like hanging out with Jep. He and I share a love for cooking and coming up with new recipes. He's the brother I would always choose first to accompany me on a road trip for a hunt or business deal. He's quieter than the rest of us, but his sense of humor is epic, and he is an awesome deer hunter. He accompanies me on many trips for deer and gets everything set up for me. I guess I have kind of prided myself on seeing value in people, no matter how big or small. When people are more outspoken about their talents, anyone can see the value, but for others you have to help them along to really unleash their potential. And, hey, life is too short to spend it with boring people. Jep and I have the same spirit of adventure. When we travel, Jase and Phil will just sit in their rooms, eat some ham and cheese, and do nothing. Jep and I always need to kick it up a notch.

Once on a duck-hunting road trip in California, Jase, Phil, Si, and the rest of the crew were gonna stay in this nasty little house with no TV and eat ham sandwiches every day. Jep and I refused and went to a casino to get a room. The best part was the casino had only one room left, and it was a suite and was the nicest one in the joint. The bad news was it was only available for one night. We took it. I went down to play a little poker to see if I could win enough money to pay for the room. Well, that didn't go like I planned. When I got back to the room, Jep was sitting in the oversized bathtub that was right in the middle of the main room, watching TV. We laughed so hard because we had never seen a bathtub in a living room before. We sat up half the night laughing about the other guys in that awful house while we lived it up. When they kicked us out the next day, we had to go find another place, and it was the worst motel I have ever stayed at in my life. The owners lived in the room behind the front desk. When I went to get ice, one of their kids got it out of their personal fridge. We went from the penthouse to the outhouse, but it sure beat sleeping on the floor at a crappy house with no TV. That's why I love running with Jep. When I feel like doing something crazy, he asks no questions and just says, "I'm in."

Korie: Jep and Jessica have four precious kids. They had three girls, Lily, Merritt, and Priscilla, then Jep had the boy he was hoping for, River. Bella and the girls love to play together. Mamaw Kay has the little girls spend the night together often and they have the best time, playing school, restaurant, or whatever. I think no matter how old our daughters get, we'll still call them the "little girls." And River is so cute with our Will. He looks up to him and thinks he's the best big cousin, and Will lets him play with all of his big-boy toys.

My oldest brother, Alan, only recently started working for Duck Commander. After high school, Alan moved to New Orleans and found some trouble. A guy beat him up with a crowbar and messed him up pretty badly. He moved back to Monroe and worked for Duck Commander for a few years. Kay and Phil always talk about how important Al was to the early years of Duck Commander. He and his wife, Lisa, lived in a little house right beside Phil and Kay's that later became the Duck Commander office for a while. Al and Lisa both worked for Duck Commander and helped to get it off the ground. Al eventually decided to go to seminary school and started working for a local church. Alan has been an incredible preacher for our church for nearly twenty-five years. He's still preaching and teaching now when he can, but it's great to have him back in the family business. When we started growing exponentially when *Duck Dynasty* came along, Korie and I started thinking about who we would need to hire to help us navigate the next steps and Alan was the only one who came to mind. We knew he was the missing piece to the puzzle. It's great to have all the brothers working at Duck Commander once again!

Alan's oldest daughter, Anna, has been working with us since she was in high school. After she graduated, she started working full-time and helps in shipping. Her husband, Jay, was a teacher and coach at a high school and up until this year he only worked for us in the summer. But we became so busy that we needed more guys who could build calls. Jay is a good hunter and has a knack for putting the calls together. If you have that skill and are kin, you got a good chance of being a Duck Commander employee.

Korie: I always say that what's worked well between the Robertson brothers is that none of them wants to do what another brother is doing, nor do they think they *can* do what another one is doing. There's no way Willie could do what Jase does. Willie doesn't have the patience to sit in a chair every day. It's not his personality. Willie couldn't do what Jep does, either. Likewise, Jase doesn't want the responsibility that Willie has because he wants to spend a lot of time hunting and fishing. He doesn't want to travel all the time going to the business meetings like Willie does. They all value each other's talent, and they each have their own special skills. Willie uses the team analogy, but I think of it like a band. If you take out one of the instruments, the song just doesn't sound as good. Everyone has their roles and they are all equally valuable. Thankfully each one really respects the others' roles in the group. Otherwise, working together would not be fun. I think what Willie brought to the family business was energy, innovation, direction, and motivation, which are attributes that a leader has to have. But Willie knows he couldn't have gotten Duck Commander to where it is today without his parents, brothers, and everyone else working for the company. A good band doesn't just consist of the lead singer.

Of course, Phil's brother, Si, has been working with us forever. Si served in the army for twenty-four years, including a stint in Vietnam. When Si retired from the army, he started putting reeds together for the calls. One of the first things I did when I took over Duck Commander was to look at our efficiency and our workload to see where I could eliminate waste. I found out Si was taking naps every day on Kay's couch! I went to Phil and told him it was a problem.

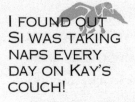

I FOUND OUT SI WAS TAKING NAPS EVERY DAY ON KAY'S COUCH!

"Look, I know he's your brother and he's my uncle, but he's not the kind of worker we need to have," I told Phil, while trying to make a good first impression.

I was trying to instill a new work ethic and culture in Duck Commander, and I couldn't have Si sleeping on the job!

"Don't touch Si," Phil told me. "You leave him alone. He's

making reeds and that's the hardest thing we do. Si is the only guy who wants to do it, and he's good at it. Si is fine."

Amazingly enough, in the ten years I've been running Duck Commander, we've never once run out of reeds. Six years ago, Si suffered a heart attack. He smoked cigarettes for almost forty years and then quit after his heart attack, so we were all so proud of him. Even before his heart attack, I wasn't sure about putting Si on our DVDs because I thought he would just come across too crazy. He cracked us up in the duck blind and we all loved him, but I told Jep and the other camera guys to film around him. Honestly, I didn't think anyone would understand what he was saying. When we finally tried to put him on the DVDs, he clammed up in front of the camera and looked like a frog in a cartoon just sitting there. He wouldn't perform. Finally, we put a hidden camera under a shirt on Si's desk. We were near the end of editing a DVD and showed a shooting scene to Si. He always takes credit for shooting more ducks than he really did. He's said before that he killed three ducks with one shot! We were watching the patterns hitting the water, and Si started claiming the ducks like he always does and going off on one of his long tangents. After we recorded him, we ran the DVD back and showed it to him. I think Si saw that he was actually pretty funny and entertaining if he acted like himself. We started putting Si on the DVDs and he got more and more popular. Now he's the star of *Duck Dynasty*!

Even though Si still takes long naps every day, he's making up for it on our DVDs. The naps don't bother me as much anymore, either, because I usually get back one-third of his pay-check in our Friday-night poker games. We begged Si to play poker with us for a long time, but he would never play because he said he loved it too much. Once Si finally showed up at our game, he never stopped coming. I guess he really does love poker that much. His wife, Christine, loves the fact that Si is getting out more and she's so proud of him. Si has one daughter, Trasa, and a son, Scott. After his heart attack, he decided he was going to start having a lot more fun and saw the bigger picture. In all the years Si has worked for us, never once has he ever really complained. He'll go off on his little tangents, but he's never come to me with a real gripe or a complaint. Phil has often said that Si is one of the best men he's ever seen. He's right; Si is as good as gold.

Some of my best friends work for us, too. Justin Martin, or Martin as we call him, played football at West Monroe High School. I pick on him, joking that he's the only man I know who looks dumb but is really smart and looks old but is really young. If you've seen him on the show, you know exactly what I'm talking about. He only lacks his thesis to complete a master's degree in wildlife biology, and he had a full scholarship to college. Martin is actually the only employee we have who ever worked in a sporting goods store that sold hunting products. He understands competitive pricing and inventory. I met Martin when he came to play poker at our house one Friday night. While on summer break from college, Martin was looking for some work. I was going out of town the next week, but I told him to come in and start calling sporting goods stores. About three days later, I received an e-mail from martin@duckcommander.com. The guy already had a Duck Commander e-mail with his name on it! I really thought he was only going to be with us for a few days and then go back to what he was doing. I never really hired him; he just ended up staying. But Martin is an excellent hunter—which gave him an advantage—and he knows all about animals. Martin will do anything for you, and he is my liaison in the blind. I'll give him new products that companies want us to try out, and he'll come back to me with everyone's feedback. Most important, Martin learned how to make our duck calls, which made him invaluable. Plus, he's another guy I enjoy hanging out with, and what's it all worth if you can't work with people you like?

> I NEVER REALLY HIRED MARTIN; HE JUST ENDED UP STAYING.

John Godwin also works with Jase, Jep, and Martin in the duck-call assembly room. Godwin used to be in the rodeo and worked the graveyard shift at the local paper mill, which is the lifeblood of West Monroe. Godwin worked at the mill for sixteen years before he started working with us. John started going to Bible study at Phil's house and hung around long enough to get a job with Duck Commander. John is a big hunter and knows about calls. Phil has more than forty duck blinds on his property, and Godwin is the guy who sets up and organizes the decoys and makes sure everything is working properly. He's also Mr. Fix-It and can fix about anything, from the four-wheelers to the RV. But John is also smart enough to put in the accounting to Walmart and has overseen our shipping department for years. John and his wife, Paula, have been best friends with my oldest brother, Alan, and his wife, Lisa, for years. He's got a great attitude and is an overall great guy.

Paul Lewis, who was my best friend in high school, is our warehouse manager. Paul and I grew up playing basketball together, and he received a full scholarship to play at Southeastern Louisiana University in Hammond. Paul played against Shaquille O'Neal and LSU one time, and Korie and I were so excited watching him on TV. Shaq fouled Paul, and Paul made one of two foul shots. In 1995, Paul got messed up selling dope and was busted transporting drugs in Texas. He got himself into a lot of trouble and was sentenced to fourteen years in federal prison. Every Friday night while Paul was incarcerated, we got a collect call from a federal prison. I tried to visit Paul as much as I could, but they moved him to federal prisons in Arkansas and Texas, so it was hard. When Paul was released, we had him moved to a halfway house in Monroe. I told the judge from day one that Paul had a job as soon as he was released. Paul made a big mistake, but he was a great friend, and I wasn't going to give up on him. He got mixed up with the wrong people. We helped him get a truck and moved him into a trailer on Phil's land. He was married in Phil's yard, and I was proud to be his best man. He and his wife, Krystle, work for us; they have three children and they just bought a house in town.

Korie: Willie and Paul have talked about how they took two paths in life. They even spoke to a youth group at our

camp last summer about how their lives turned out so differently. They told the kids about the two paths you can take
in life, and Paul is a perfect example of what can go wrong.
But Paul is also a great example of how you can change your
life and how it's not over because you make a mistake. Paul
told the kids about how scared he was during that time of his
life. He said he had a gun and couldn't trust anybody, and
how he feared it was either kill or be killed. Willie and I have
talked about the milestones in his and Paul's lives, like the
year when our oldest son, John Luke, was born or the year
in which Willie took over Duck Commander. For Paul, those
years came and went while he was in prison. Paul's life was
put on hold for fourteen years because of a stupid mistake he
made. But he learned from all of it. His attitude is incredible,
and Paul remains one of our closest friends. We love him and
his growing family.

Mountain Man came to us in an odd way. Our air condi-
tioner was out and my housecleaner said she knew a guy who
went by the name of Mountain Man who could fix it. She and
I both shared a common interest in cooling the house down
so I told her to get him over here. She warned me: "Now, he
talks funny, but he know his air conditioners." When Mountain Man showed up, I learned she was right. The guy's speech
was slower than pouring honey in January. We became friends
and I invited him to watch while we made the pilot episode
of *Duck Dynasty*. We were trying to lift a trailer in the air to
hunt out of and I thought I could use all the redneck expertise

we could get. He impressed the producers and they thought, "We gotta get this guy on the show somehow." In that same episode, Korie was having a garage sale and Mountain Man stopped by and bought my squirrel. And so a star was born. He now hosts his own radio show and enjoys people recognizing him. I think he likes the free food the best!

I like to say Duck Commander is a lot like duck wraps. Huh? No, really, it is. It's a bunch of things that may not seem like they belong together, but when they all come together they make something spectacular. Everyone at Duck Commander brings something special to the table, and rather than fighting against one another, we complement each other. Do we have our disagreements? Of course! But we don't take away from the unique flavors each one of us brings. We are all held together by a common love for family and for ducks, but more importantly we are fortunate to share a common faith. Our faith is the toothpick that holds the entire wrap together. If it wasn't for our faith in God, I can assure you, we would fall apart.

RATHER THAN FIGHTING AGAINST ONE ANOTHER, WE COMPLEMENT EACH OTHER.

How do you make a duck wrap? Take a duck breast, soak it well in brine, and then marinate it. You have to season it, split it, and then add in cream cheese, a sliver of real mozzarella cheese, and a half a slice of jalapeño pepper. Then you wrap it with thin (and cheap) bacon, and secure it all with a toothpick. Grill the wrap until the duck breast is medium-rare and the bacon is crisp. The finishing touch is glazing it with anything sweet. We all have our different twists and versions of it. All the employees of Duck Commander make up a great company. Some of our employees are sweet, some are spicy hot, and a few are a bit cheesy. Each one of us has our roles and jobs. When we put everything together right, we do amazing things.

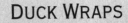

DUCK WRAPS

Simply the best way for my taste buds to eat a duck. I wrap many things, but duck has such a good flavor. Play with it and add different types of "sweets" for topping. Honey is great, but there are others. If you bite into the first one and don't think it's done, don't panic; put them all in a pot and let them steam on low fire.

½ cup salt
10 cups water
8 to 12 duck breasts
1 package cream cheese
4 to 6 jalapeños
1 package Phil Robertson's Cajun Style Rub
1 pound thin-sliced bacon
honey

1. Dissolve salt in water in a large pot.
2. Soak duck breasts in salt water overnight in the refrigerator.
3. Cut jalapeños in half (take out the seeds).
4. Cut an incision down the length of each breast and stuff with cream cheese and one half of a jalapeño.
5. Coat each stuffed duck breast with Cajun Style Rub and wrap each with one slice of bacon, securing the wrap with a toothpick.
6. Cook wraps on an open grill until bacon is crisp and cream cheese starts to ooze out (it's okay for the wrap to be medium-rare; don't overcook or it will dry out).
7. Drizzle wraps with honey and cook for an additional 2 minutes.

16

BACK STRAPS

WHATEVER YOU DO, WORK AT IT WITH ALL YOUR HEART, AS
WORKING FOR THE LORD, NOT FOR HUMAN MASTERS, SINCE YOU
KNOW THAT YOU WILL RECEIVE AN INHERITANCE FROM THE LORD
AS A REWARD. IT IS THE LORD CHRIST YOU ARE SERVING.
—COLOSSIANS 3:23–24

To tell you the truth, I *love* eating deer steak! Duck is good when you turn it into a gumbo or wrap bacon around it, but you really can't beat good ol' fried deer steak. It's so easy to make. You just cut off the back strap, soak it in milk, put it in an egg wash, add a little seasoning, coat it in flour, and then fry it up. My mouth is watering right now thinking about it. Starting Buck Commander was pretty much a no-brainer. Growing up, we did a little deer hunting so we could eat. But hunting deer wasn't Phil's first love, so we didn't do much of it. As I got older and started hunting on my own, I learned that I loved hunting deer. And like Phil, I was able to turn my passion into a successful business. After I took over Duck Commander, I was ready to branch out to something different. I knew that if I could somehow translate what we were doing with Duck Commander to deer hunting, the sky would be the limit. Let's face it: there are a lot more deer hunters out there than duck hunters.

Phil talked about getting into the deer market for quite a while, but it wasn't where his passion lay and nothing ever came of it. Jep actually did try it one time. He filmed a deer hunt, but it turned out awful. So Dad thought, "Oh well, let's just get back to hunting ducks." But I was young and full of energy and was primed and ready to start something new.

I loved the challenge of going into an entirely different market and learning everything there is to know about hunting a different species, so Buck Commander was born in 2006. For our new company to be successful, I wanted to follow the blueprint of Duck Commander. I knew hunting DVDs would be the most important products we offered. We had to produce DVDs that would make people laugh and say,

> I LOVED THE CHALLENGE OF GOING INTO AN ENTIRELY DIFFERENT MARKET.

"Wow!" at the same time. There had to be big deer, humor, and great personalities on the Buck Commander DVDs. I watched deer-hunting shows that were on TV at the time and thought much of what I saw was boring. I believed we could do better.

At the time I started Buck Commander, we were selling a ton of duck DVDs to Walmart. I thought it would be an easy transition to selling deer DVDs. Boy, was I wrong. When I tried to schedule a meeting with the deer-hunting buyer for Walmart, I couldn't even get him to return my phone calls. The big difference between ducks and deer was that Duck Commander *owned* the duck market. Deer were an entirely different beast. There was much more competition in the deer market. My whole plan seemed shot—or was it?

When Buck Commander finally got off the ground, we were able to build a great spin-off business that complemented Duck Commander. Fortunately, the Lord gave me what I was looking for—guys who were busy with their regular jobs for about eight months out of the year and then off just in time for deer season. Of all things, I found the people I needed in Major League Baseball players. Many major leaguers are avid hunters. I think it takes a lot of patience to be good at both: When you're riding a two-for-thirty slump, you have to remain patient and focused in order to hit your way out of it. When you're deer hunting, you might go three or four days without seeing a big buck. But you have to remain patient, knowing that there are some big deer out there.

Deer-hunting season takes place after the baseball season is over, so many major leaguers spend the off-season in the woods. I firmly believe that God is the one who put me with the folks I needed. My partners make a great living playing baseball in the summer, and they make some great hunting shows in the winter. I was convinced we could make better DVDs than what was already out there. I was also convinced that something as fun as deer hunting should never be portrayed as being something bland. Buck Commander set out to change things.

The first group of Buckmen included Russ Springer, who is from Alexandria (or Pollock for the locals), Louisiana, and pitched for nine major league teams from 1992 to 2010; David

Dellucci, who is from Baton Rouge, Louisiana, and was an outfielder for seven major league clubs from 1997 to 2009; and Mike DeJean, who is also from Baton Rouge and pitched for five MLB teams from 1997 to 2006. It was a coincidence that each of the first Buckmen was from my home state of Louisiana. Maybe it was because Louisiana guys are willing to take crazy chances. Word began spreading through the major leagues that something big was happening in the deer-hunting industry with baseball players, and these guys were the first ones to step up to the plate. Adam LaRoche, who was then a first baseman for the Atlanta Braves, was the next player to join the team, and he brought along Braves third baseman Chipper Jones. Chipper was a good friend of Matt Duff, who pitched for the St. Louis Cardinals in 2002, so they joined together.

Like a baseball roster, there has been some turnover with Buck Commander from season to season. My current partners are some of my closest friends: LaRoche, who is now a first baseman with the Washington Nationals; former major league pitcher Tom "Tombo" Martin; Los Angeles Angels outfielder Ryan Langerhans; and country superstars Jason Aldean and Luke Bryan.

Ryan grew up hunting deer in Texas and was teammates with Adam in Atlanta. Tombo grew up in the Florida panhandle and pitched in the majors for thirteen seasons, most recently with the Colorado Rockies in 2007. They are just really super guys who have become good friends to me over the years.

Adam is really the guy who helped me save Buck Commander and Duck Commander. Dave LaRoche, his father, pitched for the Los Angeles Angels, Minnesota Twins, Chicago Cubs, Cleveland Indians, and New York Yankees during the 1970s and early 1980s. His younger brother, Andy, was a third baseman for the Los Angeles Dodgers, Pittsburgh Pirates, and Oakland A's from 2007 to 2011. Adam was born in Orange County, California, but grew up in Fort Scott, Kansas, where there's some really big whitetail deer. Hunting and fishing have always been in Adam's blood. He loves being outdoors as much as he loves playing baseball.

When Adam was a rookie with the Braves in 2004, he lost his lucky Duck Commander hat. You know how baseball players are about their superstitions. Adam *had* to find a replacement hat. He went to the Duck Commander website and didn't find one, so he called our headquarters, and Jase answered the phone. Adam told him he was a Major League Baseball player.

"Huh, I've never heard of you," Jase told Adam. "We don't sell that hat anymore, but I think I might have one in my closet."

A couple of weeks later, Adam received a worn-out, sweat-stained Duck Commander hat from Jase in the mail. I became friends with the Rockies' first baseman Todd Helton, who is another avid deer hunter, at about the same time Adam called the Duck Commander office. Helton invited me to one of his games against the Braves at Turner Field in Atlanta in September 2005. The Braves had wrapped up their fourteenth consecutive division title the night before. Adam found out I was at the game, and I met him at home plate during batting practice. Not many people can say they met their future business partner at home plate at Turner Field.

Adam was a big hunter and told me he grew up watching Duck Commander videos. We quickly became friends and started hunting together. I was traveling a lot, getting Buck Commander off the ground, hunting all over the country with my partners and friends, Helton and other fellow Rockies players like Aaron Cook, Danny Ardoin, and Brad Hawpe.

I will never forget being on a deer hunt in Iowa with Hawpe and Ardoin. We drove through one of the worst snowstorms I have ever seen. We must have seen two hundred cars on the side of the road. You couldn't even see the exit ramps off the interstate because the snow was so heavy. It was a tense car ride. After finally making it to the camp, I got so sick I had to stay in my room the whole time. We didn't kill one deer on that trip. That's when I realized making deer-hunting videos might be a little harder than I thought!

After Adam was traded to the Pirates in 2007, Korie and I took our kids to Disney World in Orlando, Florida. We were walking around the Magic Kingdom when Adam called and told me to meet him in Tampa. He was going to drive from Bradenton, Florida, where the Pirates were having spring training. Adam had a tee time and wanted me to play golf with him. I was always up for an adventure, so I let Korie know I was going. She gave me that classic look I've seen many times before, but knew I had to go.

BACK STRAPS

Korie: We were on family vacation at Disney World with four young kids, literally in the line for Splash Mountain. Willie hates waiting in lines, so I wasn't really surprised when he jumped at Adam's offer. I had never met Adam, but I knew that Willie liked him a lot, and they had talked about his being a part of Buck Commander. While the golfing trip would be fun, it could also be an important business meeting for Buck Commander, but really? Forget the fact that I was going to be left alone at Disney World with four kids. He had to get to Tampa and we didn't have a car! Willie would figure it out, though. He always does, and the kids and I had a great time that day at the park.

I was wearing running shorts and a T-shirt. I jumped in a cab outside Disney World and told the cabbie to drive to Tampa. The cabbie started looking at his fare chart to figure out how much it was going to cost. "Turn your meter on, son," I told him. "Let's get there."

"TURN YOUR METER ON, SON," I TOLD HIM. "LET'S GET THERE."

After more than two hours in a cab, it cost me $360 to get to Tampa. Adam was standing outside this super-nice country club waiting for me with the golf pro. "This is your friend?" the pro asked. "We're going to have to get him some clothes."

I dropped another hundred dollars on a collared shirt. But the expenses were well worth it because during dinner, Adam told me he wanted to invest in Buck Commander and become a partner in the company. I was really happy to have him on board, and Buck Commander probably wouldn't have survived without him. Again, God's timing is always perfect.

When we were finished with dinner, Adam broke the news that he couldn't take me back to Orlando because he had a spring-training game the next morning and had to be at the park very early. He still had a good drive to get back to Bradenton, so I was going to have to figure out how to get back to Korie and the kids. When we couldn't find a cab to take me back to Disney World, Adam walked up to a hostess at the restaurant and offered her a hundred dollars to take me back to Orlando. He even called Korie and asked her if it was okay for another woman to drive me back.

Korie: I was just happy Willie was going to make it back. It was getting late, and I was worried he might have to spend the night in Tampa. I told Willie to hurry back and meet us at Epcot. The park was open till one A.M. that night and the kids and I were still going strong.

I ended up riding back to Orlando in an old Honda Civic with a waiter and waitress from the restaurant. The car's radio didn't even work, so these eighteen- and nineteen-year-old kids were wearing iPods, singing and smoking the entire way. I was sitting in the backseat, wondering how in the world I get into these situations. Fortunately, I arrived at Epcot shortly before midnight and was able to ride Soarin' with the kids.

Korie: I was so happy to see Willie. I was carrying Bella, who was asleep in my arms, and pushing Will in a stroller. There were still a few rides we hadn't gotten to, and John Luke and Sadie weren't ready to stop. My back was killing me, so when Willie walked up I couldn't have been more excited. I passed Bella over to him and we closed the park down!

It ended up being a really great day and set the stage for Buck Commander. It was classic Adam. I think sometimes we do this kind of stuff just so we'll have a great story to tell. He and I have had some epic adventures. In the early days, Adam and I, along with Langerhans and a few other buddies, got into a massive food/forty-ounce-drink fight outside of a restaurant chain in Texas. Adam was buying drinks at a drive-through window and was throwing them at us in the truck behind them as fast as he could!

> SOMETIMES WE DO THIS KIND OF STUFF JUST SO WE'LL HAVE A GREAT STORY TO TELL.

Adam is a great friend—he's like another brother to me. What I've learned from Adam, more than anything else, is to have *confidence.* For Adam, if you can think of it, you can do it. That motto has led to some crazy late-night arguments, where I find myself being the practical one! But I love that he's a big thinker and that he pushes me to step across that line. Adam is also a great connector. He makes friends and holds on to them. That's how Jason Aldean and Luke Bryan became involved in Buck Commander. Adam met Jason when he sang the national anthem at a Braves game in 2005. He met Luke the same year, when Adam and a bunch of his teammates went to see him play at a bar in Atlanta. They arrived after the show was over, but Luke came out and played a two-hour set just for them.

Growing up in the South, Luke and Jason have both always been hunters. Jason grew up in Macon, Georgia, and started pursuing a music career immediately after high school. Luke grew up in Leesburg, Georgia, and is not only a great singer and performer but also an awesome writer. Now Jason and Luke are both producing platinum albums. They're pretty much as big as you can get in the music industry, and I'm so happy for both of them. Jason has done everything you can do in country music. He's never afraid to take a chance and do something different. Jason does it his way, and I like that about him. I just recently surprised Luke in Nashville and showed up for his platinum party for *Tailgates and Tanlines*. In person, Luke is exactly like he is onstage: the life of the party and a blast to be around. He's also the kind of guy that really cares about his friends and has given me some really great advice as the success of the show has taken off. I don't give him the satisfaction of knowing I'm actually taking his advice, but I am listening.

On our deer-hunting trips for our show *Buck Commander Protected by Under Armour* on Outdoor Channel, Luke and Jason will pull out their guitars while we're sitting around a campfire. It's absolutely the most fun part of our time at deer camp. One of my favorite things to do is to see their live shows. Luke and Jason have put on charity concerts in Adam's hometown of Fort Scott the last few years before we go on our big hunt. It's great fun having all of our friends there together, enjoying some great music and doing something for the community. Adam and his wife, Jenn, are the kindest, most down-to-earth people you will ever meet. Korie and I are proud to have them as some of our closest friends.

Both Luke and Jason have pulled me up onstage with them all over the country. Once I took Jason his guitar during the show and knelt down, lifting it up to him with my head bowed. He was cracking up, shaking his head at me as he took it. In Little Rock one night, Luke actually offered me the microphone during a song. It may have been the only time in my life I refused an open mic, but I didn't know the song and didn't want to get up there and butcher it. Jason got me up onstage with him recently at Bayou Country Superfest in Baton Rouge, Louisiana. He asked me what song he was about to play and gave me the hint that it could have been written for my family. My mind was racing, and I sheepishly said "Hicktown." And, yes, thankfully, it was the right song. I told him next time, he oughtta give me a heads-up when he's going to call me out in front of fifty thousand people so I make sure I get it right! I still gotta get up with Jason's deejay, DJ Silver, and perform with him. It's on my bucket list.

Once my friend Colt Ford got me onstage at Rabb's in Ruston, Louisiana, and wanted me to sing a song with him. The only problem was when I got up onstage I had no idea what song he was playing. I danced and tried to fake it. The crowd's beer intake must have helped me out because I don't think they even noticed. The funny part is the song was "Dirt Road Anthem," a song Aldean took to number one later that year. When Colt came and performed in West Monroe a few years later, he called me up again. He handed me a mic and the band started playing the same song. Believe me, I didn't miss on that one! I sang most of the song from on top of a speaker about four feet in the air. It was a really fun night, for sure.

My involvement in Buck Commander has allowed me to do some pretty cool things. I go to baseball stadiums across the country to see my buddies play. I even held the finish line in the sausage race at Miller Park in Milwaukee. Earlier this year, I threw out the first pitch at a Louisiana-Monroe baseball game, which was cool to get to do at my alma mater. I was also invited to throw out the first pitch for the Mississippi Braves in Jackson, Mississippi, by my buddy Phillip Wellman, who managed them at the time. Wellman had the most classic confrontation with an umpire ever, when he crawled around the field and threw fake grenades. I pick at him all the time about that, as I'm sure all his other buddies do. He's an awesome guy.

I got to take batting practice with the San Angelo Colts in San Angelo, Texas. It's a small independent team that Tombo was pitching for when he was trying to get himself back in shape to make another run at the majors. I thought I was going to die at that game because it was 112 degrees. I realized how hard those ball players work and what good shape they are in. I had fun though, and I chased the mascot down at the end of the game. I remember thinking, "I hope this is not a girl under the costume."

The Atlanta Braves have called me a couple of times. I thought I was going to get to throw out the first pitch at one of their games, which is something I've always wanted to do. But the marketing guy asked me to sing "Take Me Out to the Ballgame" during the seventh-inning stretch. When he said that, I could feel the blood rushing out of my body, and I panicked. The guy kept talking to me, and I finally said, "Wait a second, did you just say *sing*?"

Korie told me, "Oh, you can do it. You sing all the time."

"Not to forty thousand people!" I told her.

It was "Field and Reels Outdoorsman Night" at Turner Field, so I seemed like the right choice to sing, I guess. I must have done okay because they asked me back again the next year. After the song was over, I danced on the dugout while they played "Thank God I'm a Country Boy."

The Braves brought me back the next year to sing again, and right before the opening pitch, I participated in a closest-to-the-pin golf contest with first baseman Ryan Klesko and infielder Brooks Conrad. Conrad hit his ball within about twelve feet, and Klesko hit his to about fifteen feet from the pin. I stood over my ball and could feel the blood leaving my body. I started thinking about everything that could possibly go wrong. I had a vision of shanking the ball right into the dugout and knocking Braves pitcher Tim Hudson out for the season. Before I started to swing, I told myself, "Whatever you do, don't miss this ball!" Of course, my hips flew too fast and I pulled the ball. I crushed it to where the Arizona Diamondbacks were warming up—which was nowhere near the pin—and catcher Miguel Montero caught it. That was a little embarrassing, but I thought it could have been a lot worse.

I STARTED THINKING ABOUT EVERYTHING THAT COULD POSSIBLY GO WRONG.

One time, I was meeting with my friend Lacey Biles with the National Rifle Association in Washington, DC, and Adam was playing for the Arizona Diamondbacks. I went to the game with him and was on the field for batting practice. Stephen Strasburg was pitching for the Nationals, and I couldn't wait to see Adam hit against him. I jumped the fence right before the game and was sitting in a section of seats right behind home plate. An usher told me I couldn't sit there because I didn't have a ticket. While I was arguing with the usher and trying to explain that my friend Lacey from the NRA was not there yet and had my ticket, Adam took Strasburg deep for a home run. I only saw the ball in the air. I wanted to knock that usher's teeth out. He told me I had to stand up until my ticket arrived and to not eat the food that came with the ticket. I took some joy in knowing I had already eaten three times. A few innings later, troops of soldiers came to where I was standing. They were going out on the field to be honored. Someone recognized me and invited me to stand with them, which was a huge honor. Adam told me later he looked up and saw me on a JumboTron standing with our troops.

Conversely, when I was at a Philadelphia Phillies game one time, they threw my face on the JumboTron. I covered my face with a hat when I saw it, thinking it would be funny. Of course, the fans in Philadelphia booed me. "Show your face, you blankedy-blank!" they yelled at me. You gotta love the Philly fans; they booed Santa Claus and they booed me.

In 2008, I went to St. Paul, Minnesota, to meet with Kyle Tengwall from Federal Premium Ammunition. Kyle called me and told me they couldn't find me a hotel room because the convention was in town. "What convention?" I asked him. He told me it was the Republican National Convention.

"Let's go," I told Kyle.

"Willie, you can't just go," he said. "You have to be a delegate."

"Give me an hour," I told him.

Within one hour, I had a floor pass to the Republican National Convention, thanks to my good friend Rodney Alexander, my district's congressman. While I was on the floor, several people took pictures of me, and I was starting to think I'd become a pretty big deal. What I didn't realize was that I was standing next to Mitt Romney, who was the governor of Massachusetts at the time. A few hours later my mom called me. "Willie, am I watching you on Fox News standing with Megyn Kelly?" she asked.

"Yep, who else looks like I do?" I told her.

She and Dad didn't even know I was at the convention. Kyle and I, along with Anthony Acitelli, or Ace as we call him, have had some classic trips. We've played golf at Pebble Beach in

California, attended the Masters golf tournament, and even played golf with PGA Tour pro Boo Weekley and Larry the Cable Guy. We were at the Masters, and my friend David Toms came over. Toms has hunted with us before, and we talked for like five minutes *while he was playing the Masters*! Kyle and I were cracking up at everybody's face looking at us. Right after Toms left, a guy ran up to me and asked, "Are you Gregg Allman [of the Allman Brothers Band]?" You can't make this stuff up.

Of all the crazy experiences, though, the one that really sticks out happened south of Nashville in a Walmart parking lot. My buddy Carter Smith and I took an RV to a hunting show. Carter dropped me off at Starbucks and went to Walmart for supplies. We planned to meet back at the RV. Now, if you've seen our RV, you know it has our pictures all over the side of it. I had a bag of stuff I'd bought and a cup of coffee. But when I got back to the RV, I realized Carter locked it and I was going to have to wait until he came back. I sat on the curb and waited. A guy pulled up to me and said, "Hey, man, you okay?"

"Yes, I'm good," I said, though I was a little confused.

"You need anything? Food or anything?" he asked.

Finally, I realized he thought I was homeless or just down-and-out. I'm sure my long, scraggly hair and beard were his clues. I just started smiling, and he finally looked over at our RV.

"Is that your picture on that RV?" he asked.

"Yep, I'm waiting on my driver," I said.

"I guess you are all right then," he replied.

I took no offense at his thinking I was homeless. He was a nice, kindhearted guy who thought I might be in a bad spot.

I guess no matter how big-time you think you are, there's always someone there to remind you that you're not too far off from looking like a homeless person, or maybe even one of the Allman brothers!

HE WAS A NICE, KINDHEARTED GUY WHO THOUGHT I MIGHT BE IN A BAD SPOT.

I've told you these stories not to say, "Look what I've done," but to say, "Look what God's done." I give Him all the glory. From being a kid who was on free lunches to today, a lot of good things have happened in my life. I've had a few tough times as well, but mostly I'm just happy to be here. I look around and think, "Wow, I'm eating the back strap off a monster deer that I killed in Kansas hunting with my best buddies." Life is good!

DUCK COMMANDER
KITCHEN

FRIED BACK STRAPS

This one is a simple one. Hard part is getting the meat, but that's also the most fun part. Back straps, for all you yuppies, are the back meat on the deer right along the spine. When cleaning a deer, it's the easiest part to cut off, so go ahead and do this the same day you harvest your deer. When my children find out I got a deer, they know I will be frying that night, no matter what time it is. If the deer is old or mature, you can add a step to make it very tender.

1 back strap
milk (enough to cover the meat)
a few shakes of Worcestershire or any meat marinade (we have our own)
2 eggs, beaten
2 cups flour
peanut oil (enough for 4 inches in the pot; make sure meat is covered)
Phil Robertson's Seasoning to taste

1. Cut back strap into thin steaks the width of your pinkie.
2. Mix milk and marinade and put in a plastic bag or bowl with back strap.
3. Put in fridge for an hour or two. (I shake up the bag during the process.)
4. Pull pieces out of bag or bowl and pat dry with paper towel.
5. Wash in egg.
6. Dip in flour.
7. Place in hot peanut oil; fry until brown.
8. Season with Phil Robertson's Cajun Style Seasoning as soon as it comes out of the grease
9. Taste. If it's good and tender, make your sauce (recipe follows), dip, and go ahead and eat. If tough, then do this:

   • Stack in big black skillet with onion, mushrooms, garlic, and sausage if you're feeling sassy.

- Put in oven at 300 for around 45 minutes. Should be very tender.

My super-special, super-simple back strap sauce:

    1 cup of mayonnaise
    2 squirts of mustard
    1 shake of Worcestershire
    1 teaspoon of horseradish (or more if you want it spicy)
    Simply mix these ingredients together to make the sauce.

17

DUCK AND DRESSING

"I LOOKED INTO IT AND SAW FOUR-FOOTED ANIMALS OF THE
EARTH, WILD BEASTS, REPTILES AND BIRDS. THEN I HEARD
A VOICE TELLING ME, 'GET UP, PETER. KILL AND EAT.'"
—ACTS 11:6–7

Nowadays, people often ask me what it's like hunting with my dad. We've actually had offers of tens of thousands of dollars from people who want to spend a day in Phil's blind. It always amazes us because when we were growing up, duck hunting was our everyday life. When we were kids, we were always in the blind with Dad. I don't remember my first hunt or the first duck I killed, like other young hunters. It was a different time and Phil wasn't exactly a traditional dad. He didn't take pictures of our first duck. It wasn't sentimental; it was just life. We hunted and fished because we wouldn't eat if we didn't. Phil's number one concern was always safety. If you were careless with a loaded gun, you would not come back to the blind. You'd be stuck at home with Mom the next time.

Also, you had to be prepared because Phil wasn't gonna baby you out there. If you didn't wear the proper clothes, you were gonna freeze your butt off. And I did many times! You had to get your stuff together as well: shells, guns, and whatever you needed. I will never forget a time when I was about ten and we were all going on a dove hunt. It was opening day, and we were all excited. I was shooting a .410 shotgun, but I could only find one shell. Since we were leaving early in the morning, Phil let me know we wouldn't be able to stop at a store because none of them would be open that early in the morning.

"You better make that shot count," Phil told me.

So I shadowed Phil during the entire hunt, watching him drop 'em. I ran to fetch the birds for Phil, and if any were still alive, he would pinch their heads. With one flick of Phil's wrist, the dove's head separated from its body. I was fascinated and yet a little freaked out. You can't be sensitive when you're hunting with Phil. I kept throwing my shotgun up to shoot, but I knew I had only one shot. Finally, about eleven o'clock in the morning, I saw my opportunity. I told Phil I was gonna take my shot. He was supportive and told me to make it count. Boom! Wouldn't you know I smoked the dove? I couldn't believe it. I went one-for-one with only one shell. As I turned to look at my dad with the biggest smile ever, I noticed he was putting his gun down. He'd shot at the exact same time. He wanted to make sure my shot counted.

"Good shot, Willie boy, put your safety back on," Phil told me.

I didn't know why the safety mattered since I only had one shell, but he wanted to instill the practice in my brain. We'll never know who hit that bird, but believe me, I told Jase that I got it for sure.

When hunting with Phil, the number one rule was always to follow the laws and regulations of the sport. He wouldn't allow anyone to do anything illegal when it came to hunting. You had to have a license, wait for legal shooting times, and respect the rules of duck hunting. And safety checks were constant—and still are when we're in the blind. Guns have to be put in a place where they will not fall over accidentally, even if a dog runs through the blind. Phil still tells us stories of when guys would come to him with one leg missing and blame their dogs for getting shot. When a dog accidentally knocks your gun down, it can step on the safety and its claws can pull the trigger. You wouldn't believe how many people have been shot accidentally. Phil even invented a safety gun boot to put in a duck blind so it would never happen to us.

As far as the duck-blind rules, they are sort of unwritten in Phil's blind. He always does most of the calling. You wouldn't dare pull out your duck call and start wailing. He'll let you call a drake whistle, but not a hen call. In fact, Jase had to wait several years before he could call with him. And you really only need about two good callers in a blind. People ask me, "Why don't you call in the blind?" I ask them, "Would you call with Phil Robertson in your blind?"

It's like pinch-hitting for Albert Pujols. It doesn't make sense when you have the best duck caller in the world in your blind. The benefits of not screwing up are better than those of taking a chance on doing something stupid. Believe me: if you mess up, you're going to hear about it. I never will forget when we had about twenty-five mallards almost in the hole. They were on their third pass down when the text message alert on my phone went off. After my phone buzzed, the mallards decided not to come in. Phil looked down the row of guys with a look that was a mixture of craziness, agony, and Satan himself.

"What was that?" he hollered.

Now, there was no way I was gonna fess up.

"I heard something!" Phil yelled again.

I didn't feel like trying to explain to him that there was no way the ducks heard my phone from sixty yards away, so I didn't say a word. I'm glad waterboarding isn't allowed in the blind, because ol' Phil would have filled our faces with water to find the culprit. There is always a lot of pressure to have 100 percent success. If we get four out of six ducks, we'll sit there and debate for the next two hours why we didn't get all six.

Most of the quality time I spent with my dad was in the duck blind. When I was young I didn't appreciate what it took to be so successful at the sport. We just knew that it was what Dad loved and you had to respect that. No matter what the weather was like, whether it was rain, sleet, or snow, Dad was out in the blind. I didn't hunt nearly as much when I was in high school because I was into sports and girls. It wasn't until I came home from college that I really started to understand how special duck hunting is. I grew up in and around the business of duck hunting, so it wasn't as cool for me as it was for other guys.

MOST OF THE QUALITY TIME I SPENT WITH MY DAD WAS IN THE DUCK BLIND.

My most memorable hunts happened when I was older. We were in Arkansas one year, and it was a slow day. I talked Phil into moving to an area where we saw ducks going down. We decided to take a small crew—Phil, Jase, a camera guy, and me. The mallards were pouring in like we had been seeing all morning, so we didn't even have to call that much. It was just one of those spots where the ducks wanted to be. We each grabbed a cypress tree and spread out. We limited out in like twenty minutes, all green heads! It was a special hunt.

On another memorable hunt, a lone mallard came in. Jase told Phil, "Let's let Willie take this one." Now, I know why he said it. Jase was convinced I would raise my gun and miss. Well, I raised my gun and folded it. Phil looked at Jase and said, "Ol' Willie's been practicing." We laughed and talked about my shot the entire morning.

My favorite duck is an American wigeon. I just think they are prettiest. We don't get a whole heck of a lot of them on our land in Louisiana, so we went to New Mexico to do some duck hunting. We scouted in the mornings on bluffs and looked at the potholes to see if they had birds in them. If we found ducks, we made our way down and hunted them. We found tons of wigeon there, and I loved it. It was a different type of hunting; we all like being in different environments. We also saw sandhill cranes, and those suckers came down like helicopters. Phil tried to bite their heads and that was a mistake. Sandhill cranes' heads are much harder than the heads of the ducks Phil was used to. He nearly broke his teeth! But let me tell you something, they are some of the best birds I have eaten in my life. They call them the "rib-eye of the sky," and they're right. I also went and visited the UFO Museum in Roswell, New Mexico, while we were there. I couldn't talk Jase or Phil into going with me, so I took our camera guy Jeremy Helm. It was, well, let's just say, strange.

We mostly duck-hunt in Northeast Louisiana in flooded timber. Phil has always believed a duck in flooded timber is the hardest duck to hunt. Usually, they've already fed and are looking for a place to sit and rest. Of course, there are a lot of other things that can get them in the timber besides us, so the ducks are always a little skittish.

Honestly, hunting in the timber is the only way we could have filmed our DVDs all these years because it allows us to hide our equipment. I don't think people realize how much equipment and personnel we have to hide when we hunt. There are sound guys, wires, camera guys, directors, gaffers, and a whole bunch of other equipment. We stick people in trees and anywhere else where we can hide them. Plus, one of the things we always try to capture on film is a duck with a background. Think about when you look up and the sky is your background; you lose perception on how far away everything is. But when there is a tree behind the duck you can tell the distance a lot better. If we shoot a duck at twenty yards, it looks like forty yards on TV. So we have to get the ducks as close to us as possible because it looks the best and it also helps your chances of getting them. We don't do much pass shooting. It's fun, but it doesn't look good on film; the ducks look like little dots. It's way more fun trying to get a big group hovering over your decoys—and it looks better on film too. But it's hard because the closer the ducks get to you, the harder it is to get them to commit. A duck has way better eyesight than a human. You gotta remember they came down all the way from Canada, so by the time they get to Louisiana, well, they've seen just about everything.

If you've ever been duck hunting, you know there's a lot of idle time involved in the sport. You're basically at the mercy of the ducks, weather, and God. Being Robertsons, we figured the best way to spend our free time in the blind is by cooking. There's only one chef in the blind, and several of us take turns. Everyone tries to outdo everyone else when it comes to cooking. Phil likes to say that everything tastes better in the blind—even sardines. Over time, as the blinds got bigger and bigger, so did the kitchen. Now we have a fully operational kitchen in the blind we call the "Big Blind," complete with a cooktop, boiler, and mini fridge. Most of the time, breakfast includes eggs, bacon, biscuits, and mayhaw jelly. But that's only the start. On

BEING ROBERTSONS, WE FIGURED THE BEST WAY TO SPEND OUR FREE TIME IN THE BLIND IS BY COOKING.

other occasions, we've eaten deer, dove, quail, ham, pot roast, steaks, and spaghetti for lunch in the blind. We even boiled Alaskan king crab legs one time. It's a wonder anyone came back out to shoot ducks that day.

Of course, you never know what the chef is going to come up with out in a blind. Uncle Si likes to say he's the MacGyver of cooking. Si says if you give him a piece of bread, cabbage, coconut, mustard greens, pig's feet, pine cones, and a wood-pecker, he'll make a delicious chicken pot pie! My favorite duck to eat is a wood duck, or woodie, as we call 'em. They're acorn eaters, so their meat is very clean and tasty. Most of 'em are local ducks, and they live in trees. Our place is full of 'em and you can now harvest three a day (it used to only be two). They typically fly at daylight and fly really crazy, darting and dodging to avoid trees as they fly through. They also don't fly very high in the air and stick to the treetops. Wood ducks are hard to call, although I have seen us peel 'em in from time to time. They squeal and make a noise in the air, but when they sit they have a different set of sounds. We always try to mimic the sitting sound so they think their buddies are on the water in front of us. They really don't leave the woods much, which I guess is why they have their name. They are some of the most beautiful ducks, but I just love the way they taste. They're my favorite ducks to eat hands down.

Growing up like we did is scary to think about now. We did some dangerous things; there's really no other way to say it. I shudder to think of my kids doing the things we did back then. It was a different time. I always feel like I came up in the last days of the good ol' days. Now you would never think of letting your children do what we did. There seems to be so much fear nowadays. We're concerned about lawsuits and predatory people, and I guess we know more about our surroundings and it's caused us to see danger everywhere. When I was a kid, we always rode in the back of the truck on the way home from town. No one ever thought about what would happen if we got in a wreck or if one of the kids simply fell out. I drove for years without a license. We just survived. I guess God was looking over us. He had a plan for my family. He always provided for us, and we always gave Him the glory for what we had, and we still do.

I believe our faith is what sets us apart. It's not about our beards, our success, or our hunting skills. It's the Lord. He keeps us in line. That's why we don't fight and bicker much, like a lot of families do. And when we do, we forgive one another because the Lord forgave us. That's why we don't let our own selfish desires pull us apart. We not only read the Bible and study it, but we actually live by it. We believe that what's in the Bible is the truth. We live our lives trusting that God's promises are real.

When Phil came to the Lord and began to live differently, we witnessed it happen. We saw how Phil turned his life over to God and how it changed him and our family for good. We had a crazy life growing up, but I wouldn't change any of it. My parents may not have been the best parents in the world all the time by parenting experts' standards, but they did the absolute best they could in the circumstances they were in.

And despite the obstacles, they set the bar high for us. I am so proud of them and all they've accomplished. I am proud of each of my brothers, and I have a super relationship with each

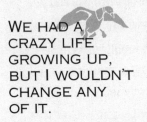

of them. I really love getting to see them every day at work. I realize that so many people will never know what that's like.

WE HAD A CRAZY LIFE GROWING UP, BUT I WOULDN'T CHANGE ANY OF IT.

I am the most proud of my children and my wife, Korie. Without her, none of this would have ever happened. She took a chance on a cute boy with dimples in whom she saw potential. Our life together has never been boring. We endured hard times with hopes and dreams of doing the inconceivable. We were content when we had very little and when we had a lot. Our kids are strong, spiritual, and well disciplined. They will have their hopes and dreams as they grow, and I will be right there beside them cheering them on.

Sure, the Robertson family has its flaws, but we're pretty good at quite a few things—like duck hunting, frog catching, fishing, and selling worms. But most important, we're really good at being a family. Like I say in one way or another at the end of each episode of *Duck Dynasty,* at the end of the day, we're a family first, and everything else is just not worth getting that worked up over.

We've enjoyed showing our family to the world through the TV screen. Best of all, it's actually fun for us to watch the show, because the Robertsons always find a way to laugh at themselves. We're the ones laughing the hardest when one of us does something stupid, which, as you can see, happens quite often!

My advice is: Don't take yourself too seriously, laugh a lot, enjoy your time with family, and appreciate the unique talents of others. Trust in God, love your neighbor, say you're sorry, forgive, and work hard. Sit down to a good meal, turn off your cell phone, respect your elders, and, of course, get out in the woods and enjoy some good ol' frog legs. That's the Robertson way!

DUCK AND DRESSING RECIPE

A classic at the Robertson household, this is our Thanksgiving meal at Phil and Kay's house. Ducks are as fresh as daylight that same morning. It is a hard one to perfect. We only eat this a few times a year, and not because we don't love it; we just do it for special occasions. If you don't have any ducks, try this dressing with turkey next Thanksgiving. I promise it'll be the best you've ever eaten.

5 or 6 ducks
salt and pepper to taste
1 bay leaf
8 hot dog buns
2 bundles green onions
1 bell pepper
2 celery stalks
1 stick butter
a 9-by-12-inch pan of cornbread
1 sleeve of saltine crackers
2 eggs, whipped
½ cup evaporated milk
1 teaspoon sage
Phil Robertson's Cajun Style Seasoning Original

1. Place cleaned ducks into a large pot. Then add salt, black pepper, and bay leaf, and fill pot with water. Boil for 2½ hours.
2. Bake hot dog buns for 2 hours at 225 degrees.
3. Dice green onions, bell pepper, and celery. Sauté your vegetables in half of the butter on medium-low heat.
4. After your hot dog buns are done, take a very large roast pot and dump your buns, cornbread, and saltine crackers into the pot. With your hands, crumble the bread mixture into a fine consistency.
5. When your ducks are done boiling, remove them from the pot and pour a third of the broth into crumbled bread mix.
6. Stir until it reaches a paste consistency. Add vegetables.

7. Add broth until you get a thick but pourable consistency.
8. Add eggs and evaporated milk to your dressing mix and stir.
9. Add sage.
10. Place ducks lightly on top of dressing. Sprinkle Phil Robertson's Seasoning on top of ducks. Lightly coat ducks with rest of butter.
11. Bake duck and dressing at 375 degrees for 25–30 minutes.
12. Enjoy!

Acknowledgments

We feel blessed beyond measure to have been able to put our life into a book. Really, how many people get to do that? It doesn't just happen, though. Our sincerest thanks to John Howard, not only a great father and father-in-law, but also an excellent book agent who knew we could do it and helped us work through this process with lightning speed. We want to thank our editor and friend, Philis Boultinghouse, who sweetly encouraged us along the way. Also Amanda Demastus, who kindly kept us on schedule, not always an easy task. Thanks to Mark Schlabach, who helped with the writing process. A special thanks to our assistant, Angila Summitt, who, along with the other things she does for us daily, helped us gather and choose the pictures to include in the book. Narrowing your entire life to just forty pictures is tough! Thank you to A&E for believing in us and allowing us to show our crazy family to the world. Thanks to our children for being patient while we added one more thing to our already busy lives. Thanks to our big family: our brothers, sisters, aunts, uncles, nieces, nephews, and cousins with whom we are blessed to be able to work hard and play hard. And last but certainly not least, thanks to our parents who gave us this story with a life well lived and who continue to be an integral part of our story and our lives. We couldn't do it without you.